A Student's Guide to

NATHANIEL HAWTHORNE

A Student's Guide to

NATHANIEL HAWTHORNE

Mary Ann L. Diorio, Ph.D.

Enslow Publishers, Inc.

40 Industrial Road	PO Box 38
Box 398	Aldershot
Berkeley Heights, NJ 07922	Hants GU12 6BP
USA	UK

http://www.enslow.com

Library of Congress Cataloging-in-Publication Data

Diorio, Mary Ann L.
    A student's guide to Nathaniel Hawthorne / Mary Ann L. Diorio.
        v. cm. — (Understanding literature)
    Includes bibliographical references (p.) and index.
    Contents: "The magnetic chain of humanity"—Life in New England—Infinite
solitude—A romantic novel—Haunted by the past—Faith and sin—Crimes
against nature—War of the heart and mind—Old and new worlds—Closing the
circle—Chronology.
    ISBN 0-7660-2283-8
    1. Hawthorne, Nathaniel, 1804-1864. 2. Novelists, American—19th century—
Biography. [1. Hawthorne, Nathaniel, 1804–1864. 2. Authors, American.]
I. Title. II. Series.
PS1881.D56   2004
813'.3—dc22

                                                    2003016053

Printed in the United States of America

10 9 8 7 6 5 4 3 2 1

To Our Readers:
We have done our best to make sure all Internet Addresses in this book were active
and appropriate when we went to press. However, the author and the publisher
have no control over and assume no liability for the material available on those
Internet sites or on other Web sites they may link to. Any comments or suggestions
can be sent by e-mail to comments@enslow.com or to the address on the back
cover.

Illustration Credits: Courtesy Peabody Essex Museum, Salem, Mass.,
pp. 19, 31, 44, 47, 60; Enslow Publishers, Inc., p. 26; ArtToday, Inc., p. 11;
Reproduced from the Dictionary of American Portraits, published by
Dover Publications, Inc., 1967, p. 53; Reproduced from the Dictionary of
American Portraits, published by Dover Publications, Inc., 1967, Courtesy
National Archives, Brady Collection, p. 132.

Cover Illustration: Courtesy Peabody Essex Museum, Salem, Mass.
(inset); Corel Corporation/ Hemera Technologies, Inc./ ArtToday, Inc.
(background objects).

Dedication

To my precious daughters,
Lia and Gina

CONTENTS

"THE MAGNETIC CHAIN OF HUMANITY"

An Introduction to the Life and Works of Nathaniel Hawthorne

When John Hathorne served as a judge in the Salem Witch Trials in 1692, he had no idea the influence this would have on the course of American literature nearly two centuries later. John Hathorne was the great-great-grandfather of Nathaniel Hawthorne. The role Hathorne played in the trials—which resulted in many innocent people being put to death due to blind superstition—caused such guilt and shame in his great-great-grandson that Nathaniel eventually changed the spelling of his last name to "Hawthorne." In this way, Nathaniel Hawthorne sought to separate himself from any connection to his ancestor. Still, the guilt and shame persisted.

Thomas Jefferson had just been re-elected president of the United States when Nathaniel Hawthorne was born at 27 Union Street in Salem, Massachusetts, on July 4, 1804. His parents were Nathaniel Hathorne and Elizabeth Clarke Manning. The second of three children, Nathaniel was their only son.

When Nathaniel was only four years old, his father—a Salem sea captain and a poet of sorts—died of yellow fever in Surinam, Dutch Guinea. His father's death left Hawthorne's mother in a state of grief from which she never recovered. Her grief strongly affected her sensitive son and triggered a sadness that lasted his entire life and colored his writing with dark melancholy. This melancholy, along with the shame Hawthorne felt in regard to his ancestry, would be two key influences on the themes of Hawthorne's later works of literature.

COMMON THEMES

Chief themes of Hawthorne's fiction include alienation, ancestral sin, guilt, pride, appearance vs. reality, and isolation and its effects. His writings often illustrate the tragedy that occurs when a person is isolated from the human community. In his short story "Ethan Brand," Hawthorne describes this isolation as losing

The above illustration captures the hysteria that pervaded the Salem witchcraft trials.

one's "hold of the magnetic chain of humanity."[1] It is this hold on the "magnetic chain of humanity" that gives meaning to life. Those characters who maintain this hold find happiness. Those who lose hold of it find only misery.

Character Types

Basically, Hawthorne's characters are of two main types: those who follow their head (or intellect) and those who follow their heart. Among those characters who follow their intellect are Ethan Brand in the story by the same name, Aylmer in "The Birthmark," Rappaccini in "Rappaccini's Daughter," and Reverend Hooper in "The Minister's Black Veil." Those who follow their heart include Hester Prynne in *The Scarlet Letter*, Phoebe in *The House of the Seven Gables*, and Owen in "The Artist of the Beautiful."

The message that Hawthorne conveys through these two broad groups of character types is that those who put the intellect above the heart end in tragedy, whereas those who put the heart above the intellect find true life.

LITERARY DEVICES

Hawthorne employs a variety of literary devices in his works. Among the most common are symbolism, irony, and ambiguity.

Perhaps the most powerful of these devices is symbolism. In *The Scarlet Letter*, for example, the red letter *A* on Hester's dress is intended to mark her as an adulteress, but for the reader, the letter will come to represent much more. Its meaning will, in fact, change several times over the course of the novel. Hawthorne's deep and complex symbolism allows for a wide variety of interpretations on many levels.

literary device—*A formula in writing for producing a certain effect, such as a figure of speech (for example, a metaphor), a narrative style (first person, second person, etc.), or a plot mechanism (such as a flashback).*

These various interpretations signal Hawthorne's use of another literary device called ambiguity. Many of Hawthorne's works, particularly his short stories, are left open-ended. In

> **symbolism**—*The literary device of using one thing or person to represent another thing or person.*

other words, the reader is left to decide the actual meaning, as is the case with Hester's red *A*. Another example of a story employing ambiguity is "The Minister's Black Veil," where the minister's reasons for taking up the veil are never directly explained.

> **ambiguity**—*A literary device that leaves the ultimate meaning of the story up to the reader.*

Some of the stories in which Hawthorne uses irony include *The Scarlet Letter*, *The Blithedale Romance*, *The Marble Faun*, and "The Celestial Rail-road." In each of these stories, some superficial action belies a deeper meaning. For example, in *The Scarlet Letter*, although Chillingworth

> **irony**—*A literary device used to express an idea that is normally opposite that of the words' literal meaning.*

becomes Dimmesdale's physician, the reader knows that Chillingworth's intention is not to heal but to do harm.

NARRATIVE STYLE

Hawthorne wrote primarily in third person and often engages the reader through his use of a narrator. His descriptions are detailed and evoke vivid images in the reader's mind. His sentences are sometimes long, and his language, although colorful, often requires close attention in order to be understood. Hawthorne's narrative style may appear somewhat difficult for the modern reader, but it is certainly worth the effort to apply oneself to understand it.

HAWTHORNE'S EARLY LIFE

When Nathaniel was nine years old, he injured his leg while playing ball. The injury left him an invalid for almost three years. It also impacted his writing. During the long period of confinement following his injury, Hawthorne developed a great love of reading. He devoured the classics, including Paul Bunyan's *Pilgrim's Progress*, Shakespeare, John Milton, and James Thomson. A favorite work was Thomson's *The Castle of Indolence*. Nathaniel also read the great literature of the Bible, which profoundly influenced his work.

Some time later, the Hathornes moved to a family property in Raymond, Maine, on the shores of Sebago Lake. There the young Nathaniel discovered the beauty of nature and developed a deep love for it. In Maine, he spent countless hours hunting, fishing, and exploring the forests. Later, he was to remember the period in Maine as the happiest time of his life.

After a year in Maine, Nathaniel returned to Salem to prepare for entry into college. During this time, his vision of his destiny became clearer. In an almost prophetic letter to his mother, he wrote, "I do not want to be a doctor and live by men's diseases, nor a minister to live by their sins, nor a lawyer and live by their quarrels. So I do not see that there is anything left for me but to be an author. How would you like some day to see a whole shelf full of books, written by your son, with 'Hawthorne's Works' printed on the backs?"[2]

COLLEGE AND EARLY LITERARY CAREER

After his father's untimely death, Nathaniel came under the care of his uncles on his mother's side. Recognizing his extraordinary literary talent, they provided for his education. In 1825, Nathaniel graduated from Bowdoin College in Brunswick, Maine. There, among other things, he studied Greek and Latin. His volume of stories for children, entitled *Tanglewood Tales*, reflects the influence of his study of the classics.

While at Bowdoin, Hawthorne developed close friendships with the poet Henry Wadsworth Longfellow, future president of the United States

Franklin Pierce, future senator John Ciley, and mentor Horatio Bridge. Bridge was the first to recognize and nurture Hawthorne's literary genius. While the two were at Bowdoin, Bridge predicted that Hawthorne would be a fiction writer. Bridge also was instrumental in the publication of *Twice-Told Tales* in 1837. This work launched Hawthorne's literary career.

These prominent friends would influence Hawthorne's life for the rest of his life. They provided him with literary inspiration and job opportunities when Hawthorne's writing did not provide enough income. When Hawthorne died, Pierce was by his side.

Upon graduation from Bowdoin, Hawthorne lived a very private life for twelve years. He spent those years in almost complete solitude working as a writer. As he wrote to Longfellow, "I have locked myself in a dungeon and I can't find the key to get out."[3] In 1828, Hawthorne anonymously self-published his first novel, *Fanshawe*. Based on his college experience, the novel attracted little attention. Discouraged, Hawthorne burned all of his unsold copies.

Still, Hawthorne remained determined to pursue his dream of becoming a published author. He continued to write stories and to send them to various New England magazines. Eventually, several of these stories earned him success when they were compiled as *Twice-Told Tales*.

Although *Fanshawe* was a literary failure, it did result in Hawthorne's friendship with the writer Samuel Goodrich. This friendship brought Hawthorne out of seclusion. He took a job in 1836 as editor of the Boston-based *American Magazine of Useful and Entertaining Knowledge*. The following year, he compiled *Peter Parley's Universal History for Children*. This book was followed by a series of children's books: *Grandfather's Chair* (1841), *Famous Old People* (1841), *Liberty Tree* (1841), and *Biographical Stories for Children* (1842).

THE TRANSCENDENTALIST PERIOD

The year 1842 marked a turning point in Hawthorne's life. In that year, he was introduced to Transcendentalism and three of its chief proponents: Bronson Alcott (father of Louisa May Alcott of *Little Women* fame), Ralph Waldo Emerson, and Henry David Thoreau. Also among the group was Sophia Peabody, whom Hawthorne married in 1842. The couple eventually had three children: Una, born in 1844; Julian, born in 1846; and Rose, born in 1851.

Encouraged by some of his friends and fellow

TRANSCENDENTALISM

The term *Transcendentalism* comes from the word "transcend," which means "to go beyond." Transcendentalism taught that man was basically good and that human life went beyond the experiences of the physical world. It also emphasized individual responsibility, a theme later explored in *The Scarlet Letter* as well as in other works of the period, such as Henry Thoreau's *Walden*, Ralph Waldo Emerson's *Nature*, and Margaret Fuller's *Women in the 19th Century*. The Transcendentalists believed that humanity could become perfect on this earth (by its own power, without divine aid), thereby achieving a perfect society called a *utopia*. The Brook Farm Experiment was an attempt to create this utopia.

writers, Hawthorne joined Brook Farm. But after a short while, he realized that his view of life did not fit in with that of the Transcendentalists, and he eventually left Brook Farm. His novel, *The Blithedale Romance*, would be based on his experience there.

utopia—*A perfect place; a paradise. The word comes from two Greek words,* ou *meaning "not" or "no," and* topos *meaning "place." The term, therefore, literally means "no place," a place that does not exist.*

LATTER YEARS

After his marriage, Hawthorne and his young bride settled in Concord, Massachusetts. Later, however, after their children were born, the couple returned to Salem for financial reasons. Hawthorne's money problems

A portrait of Nathaniel Hawthorne as a young man.

THE BROOK FARM EXPERIMENT

Brook Farm was an experimental community founded by members of the transcendentalist movement. The community was established in 1841 near West Roxbury, Massachusetts, about eight miles outside of Boston.

George Ripley, a literary critic and social reformer, led the Brook Farm experiment. Brook Farm had about twenty resident shareholders, each of whom had one vote in directing the farm's affairs. All residents worked the same number of hours on the farm for the same pay. Rising debt caused the community finally to fold in 1847.

eventually forced him to take a job, in 1846, as inspector of the Port of Salem. He worked at this job for three years. In "The Custom House," the famous preface to *The Scarlet Letter*, Hawthorne tells about his experiences while working there. *The Scarlet Letter* was published in 1850 and was followed by *The House of the Seven Gables* in 1851. *The Blithedale Romance* appeared in 1852.

In 1853, Hawthorne's college friend, Franklin Pierce, became president of the United States. Hawthorne had written a biography of Pierce that helped Pierce win the election. To show his appreciation, Pierce appointed Hawthorne as United States Consul to Liverpool. Hawthorne and his family moved to England where they lived for four years. Afterwards, they lived in Italy for a year and a half.

During his stay in Italy, Hawthorne wrote his last complete novel, *The Marble Faun* (1860).

In 1860, Hawthorne returned to the United States. He spent his final years in Concord, Massachusetts, at his beloved home, *The Wayside*. His lifelong college friend, Horatio Bridge, wrote:

> This time he resumed his pen with a heavy heart. Indeed there were many sad hearts in 1860, for the black clouds of a civil strife were settling over our fair land. The fever of excitement was raging, and the pulse of the nation had quickened into a sharp, wiry throb.[4]

Troubled by the Civil War and his failing health, Hawthorne took a trip with his long-time friend and former president, Franklin Pierce. While on this trip, Hawthorne unexpectedly died in his sleep on May 19, 1864. He was staying at the Pemigewasset House in Plymouth, New Hampshire. Emerson described the possible cause of Hawthorne's death as "the painful solitude of the man—which, I suppose, could no longer be endured and he died of it."[5] Emerson's observation would imply that Hawthorne died a victim of the very alienation about which he so brilliantly wrote.

LIFE IN NEW ENGLAND

Influences on Nathaniel Hawthorne

I n his *Literary History of the United States*, Robert Spiller writes: "We can understand New England without Hawthorne; yet Hawthorne without New England we cannot comprehend."[1] Indeed, New England culture is tightly woven into Hawthorne's life and writings. Spiller points out that it is not merely the "local color"[2] of New England that Hawthorne portrays in his work, but, rather, the "subconscious mind"[3] of the region. Note, for example, the following passage from *The Scarlet Letter*:

> Amongst any other population, or at a later period in the history of New England, the grim rigidity . . . of these good people would have augured [signaled] some awful business in hand. . . . But, in that early severity of the Puritan character, an

inference of this kind could not so indubitably be drawn.[4]

SALEM

Perhaps one of the greatest influences on Hawthorne was his hometown of Salem, Massachusetts, and its people. Salem plays a major role in several of Hawthorne's works, including *The Scarlet Letter* and *The House of the Seven Gables*.

As we have seen, Salem was a very busy seaport at the time of Hawthorne's birth and during his childhood. Ships sailed regularly to distant and exotic ports, such as Sumatra, Arabia, the Spice Islands, Africa, Spain, and the West Indies. They brought back spices, sugar, coffee, dates, figs, and raisins. Hawthorne liked to walk along the wharves. He must have smelled the aromas that hung heavily in the air from all of these delightful imports.

A FATHERLESS BOY

Like many other men of this Massachusetts town, Hawthorne's father sailed the seas for a living. Because of his unexpected death when Nathaniel was only four years old, the author developed a fear of abandonment. This fear had a lasting impact on both Hawthorne's personal development and his

PURITANS

A Protestant group whose roots go back to the sixteenth century, Puritans practiced a form of Christianity that emphasized Bible reading, prayer, and preaching in church services. They also believed in the atonement of Christ as the only means of salvation.

The term Puritan was first used in the 1500s to identify a sect within the Church of England. This sect demanded that both the church and government of England be operated according to the Bible, which they believed could be used to govern all human concerns. By the late 1500s, some Puritan groups came to believe that reforming the Church of England was impossible and departed the country. One such group moved first to Holland and then, in 1620, founded the Plymouth Colony in what is now Massachusetts. This group is better known to us today as the Pilgrims. Puritans would play a strong role in shaping the religious and social development of the United States.

Over time, the word *Puritan* has come to be identified with any strict, rigid code of morality or religion. The term also is commonly applied to those social traits identified with the original New England Colonies. Chief among these traits is the exaltation of hard work—also known as the Puritan work ethic.

writing. Indeed, the theme of the orphaned or abandoned child occurs throughout much of his work. Hawthorne biographer Edwin Haviland Miller describes this theme as "the eternal conflict of father and child which Hawthorne struggled with for a lifetime."[5]

Salem also played an important role in Hawthorne's life after college. After graduating from Bowdoin, Hawthorne returned to Salem, where he spent twelve years in seclusion. He rarely left his room except for a few trips during the summer. Those twelve years were a critical time in his literary development. During that time, he self-published his first novel, *Fanshawe* (1828). He also published several stories in *The Token* and in *New England Magazine*. Hawthorne compiled these stories into a volume called *Twice-Told Tales,* first published in 1837.

SOPHIA

Among the inhabitants of Salem who most influenced Hawthorne's life were the three Peabody sisters: Elizabeth, Mary, and Sophia. These three women were a bright light in Hawthorne's otherwise dark life. They also brightened the lives of Hawthorne's two sisters, Elizabeth and Louisa. The small group enjoyed talking about the cultural and

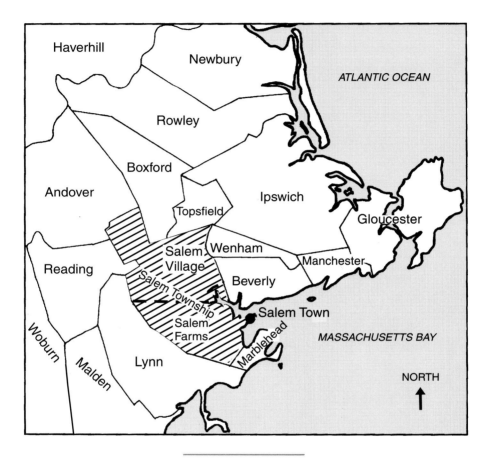

This map shows **Salem Town** and surrounding counties. Salem Town was a fishing and trading center, while Salem Village and Salem Farms were mainly farming communities.

intellectual ideas of their day, such as the progress of science and the perfectibility of the human race.

Eventually, Hawthorne married Sophia, the youngest of the three Peabody sisters. Although her poor health seemed to make her the least likely to marry, Hawthorne was drawn to Sophia. Years later, after both Hawthorne and Sophia had died, Sophia's eldest sister wrote that their marriage had been "a match made in Heaven."[6]

BROOK FARM

Through the Peabody sisters, Hawthorne was introduced to Transcendentalism and the Brook Farm Experiment. Brook Farm began in protest to the growing industrialization of the United States, which placed great emphasis on money and materialism. The three Peabody women, particularly Elizabeth, had embraced Transcendentalism and supported the Brook Farm idea. The Transcendentalists at Brook Farm wanted to create a utopian society where simplicity was the way of life.

Founded by George Ripley, a disillusioned Unitarian minister, Brook Farm covered 200 acres in West Roxbury, Massachusetts. Despite his agreement with the philosophy of Brook Farm, Emerson himself refused to become involved in the community. He claimed that he could obtain elsewhere all that Brook Farm offered.

Hawthorne, on the other hand, tried the experiment. He invested $1,000 for the purchase of two shares. Later, he regretted this purchase. He was too much of a skeptic to trust in the perfectibility of the human race. Therefore, he eventually left Brook Farm. Later, in a letter to Sophia, he described his experience there as "five golden months in providing food for cows and horses."[7]

Hawthorne's inability to embrace Transcendentalism is not surprising given his Puritan roots. Like his Puritan forefathers, Hawthorne believed in the concept of original sin. This is the belief that man is born into this world basically evil and in need of a Savior. This is directly opposed to the Transcendentalist belief that man can achieve perfection on Earth without God's aid.

original sin—*According to certain Christian theology, the state of sin that all humans are born into as a result of the first sin of the first human, Adam, who defied the will of God by eating fruit from the tree of the knowledge of good and evil.*

Through the character of Zenobia in his novel, *The Blithedale Romance*, Hawthorne appears to point out some of the inherent flaws of Transcen-dentalist philosophy. This is especially so when, at one point, Zenobia passionately attacks Hollingsworth:

"It is all self!" answered Zenobia, with still

intenser bitterness. "Nothing else; nothing but self, self, self! . . . I see it now! I am awake, disenchanted, disinthralled! Self, self, self! You have embodied yourself in a project.

You are a better masquerader than the witches and gypsies yonder; for your disguise is a self-deception. See whither it has brought you! First, you aimed a death-blow, and a treacherous one, at this scheme of a purer and higher life, which so many noble spirits had wrought out. Then, because Coverdale would not be quite your slave, you threw him ruthlessly away. And you took me, too, into your plan, as long as there was hope of my being available, and now fling me aside again, a broken tool! But, foremost, and blackest of your sins, you stifled down your inmost consciousness!"[8]

Hawthorne's main objection to Transcendentalism seems to be its teaching that people could become perfect through their own efforts. Hawthorne believed that humanity, left to itself, could never become perfect but was, instead, doomed to wickedness.

EARLY STRUGGLES

Upon his engagement to Sophia Peabody in December of 1838, Hawthorne's lack of money became a big problem. In January of 1839, through the help of Sophia's sister, Elizabeth, he got a job as Measurer of Coal and Salt at the Boston Custom House. The job, which paid Hawthorne only $1,500 a year, involved measuring the cargoes of salt and coal that entered Boston Harbor. In a humorous letter to his college acquaintance, Henry Wadsworth Longfellow, Hawthorne wrote, "I have no reason to doubt my capacity to fulfil the duties; for I don't know what they are; but, as nearly as I can understand, I shall be a sort of Port-Admiral."[9]

Hawthorne's marriage to Sophia Peabody proved to be a major turning point in his life, both emotionally and professionally. Once, when Hawthorne lost his job, he came home totally dejected to tell Sophia the bad news. In her usual, encouraging way, she told her husband not to worry. She had been saving some money, and there would be enough to sustain them for a while.

Theirs had been a slowly blossoming relationship. At first, the members of their families did not notice it. Because she was sickly, Sophia's family wondered if she would ever marry. Yet, despite her weak physical condition, Sophia secretly hoped that she would one day fall in love, get married, and have a family. Her first meeting with Hawthorne fanned that flicker of hope into a roaring flame. She wrote: "Can I ever forget when I first looked into the abyss of suns which were his eyes! And how it all grew like a flower—our love—so still, so inevitable, so consummate, and never, never to fade."[10]

Her reverence and love for Hawthorne throughout the years of their marriage gave her husband the confidence he so badly needed. Twelve years into their marriage, she wrote to her mother: "Ever since our marriage, we have always eaten off the finest

A portrait of Sophia Peabody Hawthorne, wife of Nathaniel Hawthorne.

French china—& had all things pretty & tasteful—because, you know, I would never have *second best* services, considering my husband to be my most illustrious guest."[11]

Sophia's steadfast belief in her husband's artistic talent played a major role in Hawthorne's success. Pessimistic by nature, Hawthorne often doubted his abilities and became depressed. Sophia, on the other hand, burst with optimism and hope: "I cannot be despondent, for the universe from all points, sends arrows of light into my heart & mind. I richly enjoy each thing."[12] Her ability always to see the bright side of life made Sophia the perfect balance to her pessimistic husband.

After two years at the Boston Custom House job, Hawthorne resigned in January of 1841. A few years later, in 1846, he took a position as surveyor at the Salem Custom House, overlooking Salem Harbor. The experiences he had there directly influenced his later writings, particularly *The Scarlet Letter.* The famous prologue of this novel describes the Salem Custom House in rather disparaging tones. How truly bitter Hawthorne is toward his fellow Salemites, however, is questionable. According to contemporary Hawthorne critic, Rita Gollin:

> [W]hether or not Hawthorne simply misrecollected, the discrepancy between his description

and the actuality might well have been calculated: the eagle clutches three barbed arrows (and no thunderbolts) in her left claw; but her right one holds an olive branch as well as a stars-and-striped shield.[13]

The barbed arrows juxtaposed with the olive branch would seem to suggest feelings both good and bad. Nonetheless, many of Salem's citizens saw themselves in the prologue and became angry with Hawthorne. Some never forgave him. Despite Hawthorne's seeming criticism of his hometown, however, Salem honors him today.

EARLY INFLUENCES

Among the literary influences that helped shape Hawthorne's life were the Greek and Latin classics and the works of Paul Bunyan, William Shakespeare, and Edmund Spenser. Hawthorne also read most of the works of Sir Walter Scott, as well as some of the works of Tobias Smollett, Henry Fielding, and François Rousseau.

Yet, despite the influence that the works of other writers had on him, Hawthorne's own work remains unique and marks him as the first great genius of American literature. His reputation has only increased with the passing of time.

INFINITE SOLITUDE

Major Themes in Hawthorne's Fiction

Hawthorne's works treat a variety of themes. These themes include alienation, ancestral sin, guilt, pride, hypocrisy, isolation, and the individual versus society—themes that have generated much discussion for nearly two centuries. As in all great literature, the themes in Hawthorne's works are universal. For this reason, Hawthorne's stories have endured the test of time. Although written in the nineteenth century, they deal with human emotions and problems that are common to all generations.

ALIENATION AND ISOLATION

Among the strongest themes in Hawthorne's work is the theme of alienation—the separation of a person from his larger community. This theme stems from Hawthorne's Puritan roots. His works reflect a clear and painful awareness of humanity's separation from God as a result of original sin. Hawthorne believed that every person born into this world is basically evil. In his works, he often deals with the problem of evil and with its consequences.

Closely related to the theme of alienation is the theme of isolation—when a person is not only separated from the larger community, but is also left completely alone as a result. Hawthorne's Italian novel, *The Marble Faun*, describes isolation as a consequence of being "an individual ajar with the world":

> This perception of an infinite, shivering solitude, amid which we cannot come close enough to human beings to be warmed by them, and where they turn to cold, chilly shapes of mist, is one of the most forlorn results of any accident, misfortune, crime or peculiarity of character, that puts an individual ajar with the world.[1]

In Hawthorne's thinking, being "ajar with the world" means being cut off from loving human relationships. Hester Prynne in *The Scarlet Letter* is an example of a person "ajar with the world." Isolated from the blessings of any and all friends and family, she bears the consequences of her sin alone. In the end, Hester returns to the real world by doing good to her neighbors. Although her adultery

adultery—*Voluntary sexual relations between a married person and someone other than his or her spouse.*

is never condoned, she does, nevertheless, gain acceptance and respect for her charitable deeds.

Hawthorne believed that alienation was a direct result of sin, and that sin separated a person from God and from other people. As Leon Edel has observed, Hawthorne "colored his personal drama by the larger spiritual drama of Man's dissociation from God and his divorce, through original sin, from the Garden of Eden."[2]

This larger spiritual drama pervaded not only Hawthorne's personal life, but also his literary life. Obsessed with the problem of sin, its resulting isolation, and its effects on future generations, Hawthorne fell victim to what Henry James later described as a "pressing moral anxiety."[3] As Edel states, this pressing moral anxiety "creates the profound tension below the calm surface of the often decorous and leisurely narration" of Hawthorne's writing.[4]

For Hawthorne, then, sin separated people from one another. It also could be passed from one generation to the next. Hawthorne spent his whole life struggling to free himself from the guilt of his ancestors' sins. This struggle created a continual sense of tension in his life that is reflected in his work. Unfortunately, Hawthorne never resolved this tension. His work, however, is so much the better as a result.

HYPOCRISY

Another important theme in Hawthorne's writings is the theme of hypocrisy. A keen observer of the human heart, Hawthorne had the rare ability to discern the hidden motives of people, which, in his view, often conflicted with their surface actions. Whereas most people looked only at the surface of things, Hawthorne penetrated beneath the surface. There he observed the innermost thoughts and desires of people's hearts. Hawthorne's great genius lay in being able to portray those hidden motives through the written word. One remembers his characters not so much for what they look like or what they do, but more for what they think and feel.

The character of Arthur Dimmesdale in *The Scarlet Letter* is an excellent example of the theme of hypocrisy. After committing the sin of adultery, Dimmesdale subsequently spends most of his life living a lie. On the surface, he continues to appear as a pious man of God, but, in truth, he is a sinner. The guilt he feels over this fact eats away at him and eventually destroys his health. Dimmesdale's failure to confess his sin keeps him a prisoner of it. Although he is free physically, he is not free spiritually or psychologically.

Hester, on the other hand, confesses her sin of adultery and is set free spiritually, despite the fact that she is placed in prison. Dimmesdale's failure to confess his sin while Hester bears the entire blame for it marks Dimmesdale as a hard-hearted, proud egotist. He cares more for his own reputation than for the woman and the child he has wronged.

PRIDE

The theme of pride, especially intellectual pride, also plays a major role in Hawthorne's work. Hawthorne lived and wrote at a time in history that placed increasing emphasis on science and its powers. This emphasis was a direct result of the Age of Enlightenment in the preceding century.

Human reason reigned supreme during the Enlightenment. Philosophers believed that human beings could attain happiness through the intellect alone. The intellect was exalted as the means whereby the human race would reach perfection.

Enlightenment philosophy swept Europe in the 1600s and 1700s and then made its way to the United States. Enlightenment thinking viewed history as showing steady progress and forward development in nearly all of man's endeavors. This thinking promoted the idea of progress, particularly scientific progress. People believed that this progress would continue indefinitely and that only good things would result from it.

By Hawthorne's time, a new movement called Romanticism had begun to oppose Enlightenment thinking. Indeed, Romanticism was a direct reaction against Enlightenment philosophy. Romanticism emphasized passion above reason, and imagination above rational thought.

Although not totally opposed to scientific progress, Hawthorne feared the consequences of the blind pursuit of scientific knowledge. Two of his short stories—"The Birthmark" and "Rappaccini's Daughter"—deal directly with this fear. Both Aylmer in "The Birthmark" and Signor Rappaccini in "Rappaccini's Daughter" are scientists who use their scientific knowledge to play God. In placing more importance on their intellects than on their hearts, they destroy the people they love. In the end, both Aylmer and Rappaccini are destroyed by their intellectual pride.

Romanticism—*An artistic movement of the late eighteenth and early nineteenth centuries which emphasized the imagination and emotions over rational thought. Romanticism also stressed individual freedom and rejected the restrictions of social convention.*

Like the Romanticists of his day, Hawthorne saw the dangers in elevating the intellect above the heart. In "The Birthmark," Aylmer's experiment on his wife results in her death. In "Rappaccini's Daughter," Rappaccini's experiment on his daughter results in her death as well.

True to Romanticist philosophy, most of the characters in Hawthorne's stories are primarily feeling characters, not coldly rational ones. They are moved by their emotions, not by their intellects. Hawthorne implies that those who choose to silence their hearts in order to follow their intellects end up facing tragedy.

GUILT AND ANCESTRAL SIN

Perhaps the strongest underlying themes in Hawthorne's work are the themes of ancestral sin and the guilt that goes with it. These themes grew out of Hawthorne's own family history. In fact, were it not for Hawthorne's own experience with the guilt and shame of ancestral sin, he probably would not have written many of his stories.

As we have seen, Hawthorne descended from a line of ancestors known for their stern legalism. Of particular note are William Hathorne, the first of the American Hathornes, and William's son, John. Regarding the former, Hawthorne wrote that he was "a bitter persecutor" whose "hard severity toward a woman of the [Quaker's] sect . . . will last longer, it is to be feared, than any record of his better deeds, although these were many."[5] To the latter,

Hawthorne gives a more serious indictment, writing that in John Hathorne, "the persecuting spirit . . . made himself so conspicuous in the martyrdom of the witches, that their blood may fairly be said to have left a stain upon him."[6]

legalism—*A philosophy of strict adherence to the letter of the law, even if this means ignoring the original idea or spirit behind the law.*

All of Hawthorne's works deal in some way with the author's opposition to legalism. Hawthorne critic, John W. Stuart, notes the following:

> A consideration of the images from Christianity, which he [Hawthorne] applies to victims of Puritanism . . . clearly establishes his endorsement of love, tolerance, and mercy and confirms his opposition to any rigid dogmatism that fails to appreciate the supremacy of those values.[7]

Stuart adds:

> William and John Hathorne would undoubtedly have viewed Pearl [Hester's illegitimate daughter in *The Scarlet Letter*] as more a product of the sinful world of the flesh than any rarefied one of the spirit, and they would probably classify any religious influence that Hester might potentially possess as nothing more than that of a satanic cult. Clearly, their descendant differs sharply with them.[8]

A ROMANTIC NOVEL

Examining The Scarlet Letter

The Scarlet Letter is Nathaniel Hawthorne's best known work. It is a story about the consequences of an adulterous relationship between Arthur Dimmesdale, a minister, and Hester Prynne, a young woman of the town. Hawthorne wrote *The Scarlet Letter* during the late 1840s. The novel created quite a stir when it was published in 1850 and quickly made Hawthorne a famous author.

Like *The Blithedale Romance*, Hawthorne considered *The Scarlet Letter* a "romance" rather than a "novel." He explains that a novel "is presumed to aim at a very minute fidelity, not merely to the possible, but to the probable and ordinary course of man's experience."[1] A romance, on the other hand, he felt "has fairly a right to present that truth under circumstances, to a great extent, of the writer's own choosing or creation."[2]

In other words, according to Hawthorne, a novel sticks to the facts of real-life experiences. In a romance, the author has more freedom to be creative by altering or expanding on some of those facts. C. H. Holman supports this definition when he writes, "Romance is now frequently used as a term to designate a kind of fiction that differs from the novel in being more freely the product of the author's imagination than the product of an effort to represent the actual world with verisimilitude [the appearance of reality]."[3]

A romance often relies heavily on symbolism. A symbol is something that stands for something else. It can also be a visible sign of something invisible. The main symbol in *The Scarlet Letter* is the red letter *A* that Hester Prynne wears on the front of her dress. The visible letter *A* stands for adultery (or adulteress), representing the sin that is both visible to the world and invisible in Hester's soul.

Other important symbols include the names of the main characters, which often reveal their innermost selves; the

novel—*A usually long prose narrative that deals with a particular truth of human experience.*

romance—*A long prose narrative using fantastical happenings in an attempt to connect a bygone era with the present.*

THE

SCARLET LETTER,

A ROMANCE.

BY

NATHANIEL HAWTHORNE.

BOSTON:

TICKNOR, REED, AND FIELDS.

M DCCC L.

The title page of the first edition of Hawthorne's *The Scarlet Letter* (above) proclaimed the tale a "Romance."

scaffold in the town square; the meteor that appears in the night sky; the rosebush that stands next to the prison door; and the child Pearl, herself.

PLOT DEVELOPMENT

The Scarlet Letter takes place in the mid-1600s in Boston, Massachusetts. The story starts with a famous chapter entitled "The Custom House." Like Hawthorne, the narrator once worked as an inspector at the custom house in Salem, Massachusetts. He tells about discovering in the attic of the custom house a patch of red cloth shaped like the capital letter *A*:

> My eyes fastened themselves upon the old scarlet letter, and would not be turned aside. Certainly, there was some deep meaning in it, most worthy of interpretation, and which, as it were, streamed forth from the mystic symbol, subtly communicating itself to my sensibilities, but evading the analysis of my mind.[4]

The narrator places the letter A on his chest and has a shocking emotional reaction:

> . . . it seemed to me, then, that I experienced a sensation not altogether physical, yet almost so, as of burning heat; and as if the letter were not of red cloth, but red-hot iron. I shuddered, and involuntarily let it fall upon the floor.[5]

Following this surprising reaction, the narrator discovers "a small roll of dingy paper."[6] He opens it and finds an explanation of the letter A. This explanation begins the story of *The Scarlet Letter*.

The Scarlet Letter presents the lives of four people: Hester Prynne, the Reverend Arthur Dimmesdale, Roger Chillingworth, and Hester's little daughter, Pearl. The young Hester, who is married to the elderly Roger Chillingworth, is unfaithful to him and has a child with the Reverend Dimmesdale. This child is Pearl.

Because of her sin, Hester is ostracized. She is forced to climb upon a scaffold and to stand there for three hours so that everyone can see that she is an adulteress. On the front of her dress, she wears a large red letter *A*, a reminder of her sin. Hawthorne writes: "On the breast of her gown, in fine red cloth, surrounded with an elaborate embroidery and fantastic flourishes of gold thread, appeared the letter A."[7] When questioned three times by Dimmesdale to name the man with whom she sinned, Hester refuses. This knowledge becomes her secret, a secret she will allow no one to wrench from her.

Among the crowd of people staring at Hester on the scaffold is her estranged husband. About two years earlier, he had sent her alone to America with the promise that he would join her shortly. When he failed to arrive, however, it was assumed that he had been lost at sea. It was during this time of separation from her husband that Hester committed adultery with Dimmesdale.

Hester's husband has changed his name to Roger Chillingworth and now practices medicine in Boston. When he learns of Hester's unfaithfulness to him, he decides to seek revenge.

Although the people of the town know of Hester's sin, they do not know that Reverend Dimmesdale is

The Custom House where Hawthorne once worked (above) served as the inspiration for the opening chapter of *The Scarlet Letter.*

involved in it. Indeed, because the townspeople hold Dimmesdale in almost superhuman reverence, he greatly fears confessing his sin and spends years hiding it.

But the weight of guilt takes it toll on his health. Finally, unable to bear the guilt any longer, Dimmesdale goes one night to the scaffold in the public square and shouts his guilt. At first, no one hears him. But soon, Hester and Pearl pass by, on their way home from a service at the deathbed of Governor Winthrop. Such acts of kindness on Hester's part have become a means of expiating her sin by service to the community.

As Hester and Pearl pass the scaffold, Pearl hears Dimmesdale's grim laughter. She and her mother approach Dimmesdale. For the first time, the illegitimate family is united on the scaffold. Yet, for Dimmesdale, the public cover-up continues, for he still fails to confess his guilt.

Ironically, Dimmesdale becomes a patient of Dr. Chillingworth. Chillingworth even takes up residence in Dimmesdale's house so that he can better "care" for the ailing minister. In reality, Chillingworth is suspicious that Dimmesdale's ailments are related to Hester's secret and that Dimmesdale is, in fact, her partner in adultery.

Chillingworth torments Dimmesdale with questions

and comments until the minister's anguish becomes unbearable. When Hester sees that Dimmesdale is growing worse, she asks Chillingworth to stop tormenting the sick minister. True to his cruel nature, however, Chillingworth refuses.

One afternoon, while Dimmesdale is sleeping, Chillingworth discovers a mark on the minister's breast. Hawthorne does not reveal the details of this mark to the reader. It is widely assumed, however, that the mark is in the shape of the capital letter A. The discovery of this mark convinces Chillingworth that Dimmesdale was, indeed, Hester's lover and the father of Pearl.

Upon this discovery, Chillingworth increases his torment of the minister. Some time later, Hester and Pearl meet Dimmesdale in the woods. When Hester reveals to him that Chillingworth is her husband, Dimmesdale is furious. But Hester convinces him to run away to Europe with her and Pearl. There they can start a new life together. Dimmesdale agrees, and the three plan to depart after Dimmesdale gives his Election Sermon.

To her dismay, Hester later learns that Chillingworth has booked passage on the same ship. When Dimmesdale learns of this immediately following his Election Sermon, his spirit is finally broken. He walks to the town scaffold, calls Hester and Pearl to him, and confesses his sin before all the people.

Then, in a dramatic moment, Dimmesdale rips open his shirt and reveals the mysterious mark that guilt has etched upon his own chest:

> With a convulsive motion he tore away the ministerial band from before his breast. It was revealed! But it were irreverent to describe that revelation. For an instant the gaze of the horror-stricken multitude was concentred on the ghastly miracle; while the minister stood with a flush of triumph in his face, as one who, in the crisis of acutest pain, had won a victory.[8]

At this point, Dimmesdale falls to his knees and dies.

Hawthorne called *The Scarlet Letter* a "tale of human frailty and sorrow."[9] The story deals with human weakness, the sin to which it leads, and the suffering that follows. Hawthorne shows the consequences of sin not only in the sinner's life, but also in the lives of those affected by the sin.

One significant aspect of *The Scarlet Letter* is its universal appeal. As Hawthorne's son, Julian, later noted, "All have felt the allurement of temptation, but few realize the sequel of yielding to it."[10] Therefore, "The *Scarlet Letter* is a self-revelation to whomsoever takes it up."[11]

CHARACTER DEVELOPMENT

A closer study of the four central characters of this great book reveals Hawthorne's artistic genius and his profound understanding of human nature.

HESTER PRYNNE

Hester Prynne is the main character in *The Scarlet Letter*. The story deals with the forces that shaped her and the changes caused by those forces.

Hawthorne does not tell us too much about Hester's past. We know only that her marriage to Chillingworth was arranged by her parents, and that she really did not love him. In the early chapters of the book, Hawthorne suggests that Hester was strong-willed and passionate.

Most of what the reader knows about Hester, however, comes from the picture Hawthorne paints of her life after her adultery. Spontaneous and free-spirited before committing her sin, Hester becomes thoughtful after committing it:

> Much of the marble coldness of Hester's impression was to be attributed to the circumstance that her life had turned, in a great measure, from passion and feeling to thought.[12]

Hester's passion and feeling develop into a quietly defiant pride that ultimately earns her the respect of her community. This respect is aroused, in large part, because of Hester's attitude toward herself: "Hester is thought of as a victim . . . and that isn't what she is at all."[13] On the contrary, she is a woman of great strength who acknowledges her sin and makes an effort to repair the wrong she has done. Her dedication to protecting Dimmesdale is an indication of the strength of her love for him. Moreover, her secrecy is essential to the plot development of the novel. Were Hester to divulge Dimmesdale's true identity early in the story, there would be no story.

Critic Sacvan Bercovitch goes so far as to compare Hester to the Biblical Esther whose name may have influenced Hawthorne's naming of his character: "Hester Prynne builds upon the tradition of the biblical Esther—homiletic exemplum of sorrow, duty, and love."[14] Like the Biblical Esther, Hester is concerned more about her relationships with the people she loves than with the opinions of others.

ARTHUR DIMMESDALE

Like Hester, Dimmesdale's story also deals with the forces that shaped him and his response to those forces. Once a scholar at Oxford University in England, Dimmesdale still displays many scholarly traits. He is reserved and withdrawn, and he possesses a very sensitive conscience that causes him

Julian Hawthorne, novelist, writer, and son of Nathaniel Hawthorne.

unbearable guilt. Unlike Hester, who finds freedom in confessing her sin, Dimmesdale continues to bear the burden of it alone.

He is, in essence, a selfish man. His fear of losing his good reputation is greater than his love for Hester. Julian Hawthorne writes: "Dimmesdale cares more for his social reputation than for anything else. His self-respect, his peace, his love, his soul—all may go: only let his reputation remain!"[15] Ironically, Dimmesdale's concern with upholding his false image at all costs ends up destroying him. He prefers to cling to a lie than to embrace the truth.

ROGER CHILLINGWORTH

Roger Chillingworth, as his name implies, is a cold, cruel, and manipulative man. Hawthorne tells the reader that Chillingworth was unkind to Hester in the early years of their marriage. Later, when he sends her to America, he stays behind in Europe for his own selfish purposes, thus revealing his lack of tenderness and sensitivity.

In *The Scarlet Letter*, Chillingworth represents evil in all of its ugliness. Through Chillingworth, Hawthorne shows the horrible depths to which a soul bound by malice can plunge. Bent on revenge at all costs, Chillingworth is motivated by pure hatred. His sin, therefore, seems worse than either Hester's or Dimmesdale's, who were motivated by love, albeit misguided love.

PEARL

The child Pearl is more of a symbol than a character. Her function is to act as a constant reminder to Hester and Dimmesdale of their sin. Indeed, Pearl is the fruit of that sin. As Karen Sanchez-Eppler points out, "Pearl had . . . imbibed from her mother the passion and sinfulness of the act that conceived her."[16] She represents the tragedy of unfaithfulness made flesh. In one of the novel's most memorable scenes, Pearl torments Hester with continual questions about the letter *A*: "Mother," said little Pearl, "the sunshine does not love you. It runs away and hides itself because it is afraid of something on your bosom [the scarlet letter]."[17]

By asking Hester direct questions, Pearl keeps her mother's sin ever before Hester's eyes, as well as Dimmesdale's. On the night the two discover Dimmesdale on the town scaffold, Pearl asks him to stand with them there the next day at noon. When Dimmesdale does not have the courage to do so, Pearl cries out with scorn: "Thou wast not bold, thou wast not true! Thou wouldst not promise to take my hand and mother's hand, to-morrow noontide!"[18]

Just as Pearl is the embodiment of sin, she is also the victim of it. Her obsession with her mother's scarlet letter reveals a perception that is unusual for a child of her age. This perception causes Hester at times to cringe, at other times, to drive her daughter away.

GUILT

Hawthorne explored the many sides of human emotions and their effects on people. He was especially interested in guilt and its consequences. Julian Hawthorne writes: "the controlling purpose of the story, underlying all other purposes, is to exhibit the various ways in which guilt is punished in this world."[19] In Hester's case, guilt is punished by a continual public display of it in the form of the letter *A*. In Dimmesdale's case, guilt is punished by the torments of conscience.

As the years pass, the letter *A* takes on a new meaning in Hester's life. Because she treats her neighbors with great love and kindness, they no longer look on the letter *A* as signifying "Adulteress":

> Such helpfulness was found in her—so much power to do, and power to sympathize—that many people refused to interpret the scarlet A by its original signification. They said that it meant Able; so strong was Hester Prynne, with a woman's strength.[20]

Thus, Hester reclaims herself by ministering to, or holding on to, humanity. Dimmesdale, on the other hand, only pretends to minister. Both he and Chillingworth remain isolated—having chosen to let go of their hold on the chain of humanity.

HAUNTED
BY THE
PAST

Examining
The House of the Seven Gables

Less popular than *The Scarlet Letter*, but also of major influence, is Hawthorne's novel, *The House of the Seven Gables*. This novel was published in 1851, just a year after the publication of *The Scarlet Letter*. It tells the story of the effects of a family curse placed on an ancestor of the Pyncheon family by an ancestor of the Maule family.

As its title implies, and like *The Scarlet Letter* before it, *The House of the Seven Gables* is a romance. In keeping with his definition of a romance, Hawthorne notes in the preface to this work that "the point of view in which this tale comes under the Romantic definition lies in the attempt to connect a by-gone time with the very present that is flitting away from us."[1] Moreover, the novel adheres to Romantic tenets in that it includes "fantastical occurrences, improbabilities, and attempts to connect the past with the present, sacrificing literal authenticity for more abstract truths."[2] Indeed, as we have seen, a romance differs from a novel precisely because of its fantastical elements and its departure from reality.

Critic Claudia Durst Johnson, however, refutes the labeling of the novel as a romance. She boldly puts forth the thesis that *The House of the Seven Gables* is, above all, about money:

> The central idea of this novel is money in all its permutations. Its topics are business, property, inheritance, greed, and poverty. The novel's exposition, its plot, the identification and motivation of its characters, its social context, its theoretical musings, its metaphors are economic. And the imperative that moves plot and characters is economic. Despite the author's claim on romance and spiritualizing, *The House of the Seven Gables* is fundamentally pragmatic and materialistic in a way that makes this one of his *least* rather than most romantic fictions. The conclusion, which Hawthorne readers for a century have found impossibly "golden" and romantic, is anything but romantic. It is as crass and cold-blooded as old Judge Pyncheon himself.[3]

That the work is open to such different interpretations is indicative of its richness and complexity.

Hawthorne started writing *The House of the Seven*

Gables in September of 1850, the same year in which he finished *The Scarlet Letter*. He worked on the book for nearly five months and completed it in mid-January of 1851.

> **metaphor**—*A figure of speech that suggests a comparison or similarity between two normally unrelated things.*

Considered by some to be a Gothic novel, *The House of the Seven Gables* combines what Hawthorne calls "the Marvelous" with the ordinary.[4] In other words, the story includes references to the world of curses, evil spirits, and witchcraft. This evil world springs from the sins of past generations. In *The House of the Seven Gables*, Hawthorne makes reference to his great-great-grandfather, John Hathorne, one of the three judges whose involvement in the Salem Witch Trials caused Hawthorne great embarrassment.

Hawthorne thought that, as a literary work, *The House of the Seven Gables* was better than *The Scarlet Letter*. When the book first appeared in the Spring of 1851, Hawthorne wrote to his good friend, Horatio Bridge:

> 'The House of the Seven Gables' in my opinion, is better than `The Scarlet Letter:' but I should not wonder if I had refined upon the principal character a little too much for popular appreciation, nor if the romance of the book should be somewhat at odds with the humble and familiar scenery in which I invest it. But I feel that portions of it are

The above house served as the inspiration for Hawthorne's *The House of the Seven Gables.*

as good as anything I can hope to write, and the publisher speaks encouragingly of its success.[5]

PLOT DEVELOPMENT

The story begins with a history of the Pyncheon family dating back two hundred years before the events of the book begin. Hawthorne wrote this chapter to give the reader necessary background information for understanding the rest of the story.

First he describes the house, one of the key symbols in the story. He compares the outward appearance of the house to a human face: "The aspect of the venerable mansion has always affected me like a human countenance."[6]

This comparison of the house to a human face is a theme that runs throughout the story. Just as a human face grows older, so does the house of the seven gables grow older as generations of Pyncheons continue to reside there.

The seven-gabled house sits on Pyncheon Street, at one time called Maule's Lane. Maule's Lane was named after Matthew Maule, the original owner of the property on which the house of the seven gables stands. Before the house was built, Maule's log cabin stood on the property. On the same property was a clear spring that provided fresh water and made the land very valuable. As the town grew, Maule's property caught the eye of Colonel Pyncheon, the wealthy ancestor of the characters in the story, who eventually acquired the property through dubious means.

Matthew Maule was believed to be a wizard. When he refused to sell his property to Colonel Pyncheon, the colonel initiated a charge of witchcraft against Maule. As a result of this charge, Maule was convicted and eventually killed. Prior to Maule's death, however, Colonel Pyncheon acquired the coveted property. While the house of the seven gables was being built, Maule spoke a curse on the colonel and his descendants. He said that God would give Colonel Pyncheon blood to drink because he took advantage of a poor man.

Shortly after the house was completed, Colonel Pyncheon did indeed choke on his own blood and died. The death occurred during a housewarming party to which the colonel had invited the community. From that moment on, the colonel's descendants seemed destined to misfortune because of Maule's curse upon them.

All the characters in the novel are descendants of either Colonel Pyncheon or Matthew Maule. Judge Pyncheon, a wealthy and well-respected member of the community, is greedy and cruel, like his ancestor, Colonel Pyncheon. Also like his ancestor, Judge Pyncheon dies an unnatural death, thus fulfilling Matthew Maule's original curse.

CHARACTER DEVELOPMENT

Hawthorne builds his story around the lives of six important characters: Hepzibah Pyncheon, Clifford Pyncheon, Phoebe Pyncheon, Judge Jaffrey Pyncheon, Colonel Pyncheon, and Holgrave.

Hepzibah and Clifford are brother and sister. Phoebe is their young cousin. Judge Jaffrey Pyncheon is an older cousin who resembles their ancestor, Colonel Pyncheon, both physically and morally. Holgrave is a young man who rents a room in the house of the seven gables. He is a direct descendant of Matthew Maule, who spoke a curse on Colonel Pyncheon. Although Colonel Pyncheon has been dead for almost two hundred years, he still exerts a powerful influence over all the other characters. A minor character, Alice Pyncheon, falls victim through pride to the Pyncheon family curse. Two lesser characters, Uncle Venner and Ned Higgins, add humor to an otherwise somber tale.

Hawthorne uses symbolism in the creation of his characters. This means that each of his characters represents an aspect of life or of society.

Hepzibah is a sixty-year-old unmarried woman with a good heart but a sour-looking face. Her eyesight is poor and causes her to squint continually. Because of this, she looks as though she is always angry when, in fact, she is not.

Hepzibah is not, however, a happy woman. She has been grieving for her brother Clifford. As the story opens, Clifford is in prison for killing an uncle twenty-five years earlier. But Clifford did not commit the crime. The murderer is Judge Jaffrey Pyncheon, cousin to Hepzibah and Clifford. Judge Jaffrey Pyncheon has become a rich, influential figure in the town, a fact that causes Hepzibah deep distress.

Due to her poor financial situation, Hepzibah is forced to open a little store, called a "cent shop," in order to support herself. A "cent shop" is a kind of general store where customers can buy items such as flour, sugar, apples, beans, soap, and candles, among other things (comparable to a dollar store today). Having grown up in wealth, Hepzibah is embarrassed at having to open a store to earn a living. Because she has lived alone and out of touch with the world for such a long time, she has difficulty relating to her customers.

Hepzibah is a symbol of the dying upper class of society. During Hawthorne's day, the aristocratic class was becoming less and less influential as the new middle class began to take a more important place in society. Hepzibah represents this dying aristocratic class.

Clifford, Hepzibah's brother, symbolizes isolation from society and the consequences of such isolation. Having been wrongfully imprisoned for the murder of his uncle, Clifford eventually is released and returns to the house of the seven gables.

Thirty years have passed since his imprisonment. During those years, Clifford has become a man isolated from society and isolated even from himself. Hawthorne describes him as follows: "Continually . . . his mind and consciousness took their departure, leaving his wasted, gray and melancholy figure—a substantial emptiness, a material ghost—to occupy his seat at table."[7]

But this "ghost" of a man has a saving gift, the ability to appreciate beauty. He is keenly aware of the beauty around him, particularly that of his young cousin Phoebe, of whom he grows very fond. Her beauty draws Clifford out of himself to some degree and provides him with a taste of happiness.

Clifford is an expression of Hawthorne's belief that happiness is found not in isolating oneself from other people, but in joining oneself to them. Only when Clifford tries to become a part of society again does he experience some of the life that he had lost.

Phoebe, the seventeen-year-old cousin of both Clifford and Hepzibah, is a descendant of a branch of the Pyncheon family that settled in Maine. Hawthorne named Phoebe after the pet name he called his wife Sophia. Indeed, the character of Phoebe is most likely based on Sophia. Phoebe, whose name means "radiant," is a cheerful young girl who spreads love and light all around her, much as Hawthorne's wife did. Phoebe is also simple, honest, and innocent. By her presence, she transforms the atmosphere of the house of the seven gables and the people in it. When she leaves for a few days to go back to Maine to visit her family, the house and the people in it return to their negative appearance and attitude.

As a symbol, Phoebe represents redemption. In a very real sense, she is the "savior" of the Pyncheon family. She rescues them from the darkness of evil and leads them into the light of goodness and grace.

Judge Jaffrey Pyncheon is the much-despised cousin of Hepzibah and Clifford. It was he who supposedly framed Clifford, causing him to be wrongly imprisoned for the murder of an uncle.

Judge Jaffrey Pyncheon, a hypocrite, represents evil disguised as good. Hawthorne calls him the "original Puritan" because he so closely resembles the original Colonel Pyncheon, ancestor of the cursed family.[8] Indeed, when Phoebe meets Judge Pyncheon for the first time, she is struck by his resemblance to "the progenitor of the whole race of New England Pyncheons."[9]

Not only does Judge Jaffrey Pyncheon look like his ancestor, he acts like him. The many similarities between the two men reflect Hawthorne's continual concern with the influence of past generations on present ones. The similarities also reflect one of Hawthorne's most important themes, the theme of appearance vs. reality.

Holgrave, the daguerreotypist who lives in the house of the seven gables, represents progress. According to Melissa Pennell, Holgrave "frequently questions the aristocratic sensibility of Hepzibah Pyncheon and expresses his desire to escape the past, its influence and legacy."[10]

A descendant of Matthew Maule, Holgrave possesses his ancestor's evil powers. When tempted to use those powers against Phoebe, however, he resists the temptation because of his love for her. In this he displays an element of nobility. His action also hints at the idea that ancestral sins do not have to be repeated if they are resisted by subsequent generations.

At the same time, Holgrave is an ambivalent character. Early in the novel, the reader sees him as a man of action bent on promoting the cause of the common man. By the end of the story, however, Holgrave seems to have embraced those very things he opposed earlier. This ambivalence makes Holgrave's actions at the end of the story seem somewhat contrived:

daguerreotypist—*A person who engaged in the early photographic process of producing daguerreotype (photographs on a silver or a silver-covered copper plate).*

> The seeming change in Holgrave's character at the end of the novel has troubled many readers. Not only

does he reveal himself to be a Maule descendent, but he embraces the ideas about property and status that he had rejected earlier in the novel. Hawthorne has hinted that Holgrave has an attachment to the land through his gardening, but the ideas he expresses late in the novel about building a house that will last strike some readers as artificial. Holgrave also appears ready to abandon his art for the life of a country gentleman-farmer, another change that readers find disturbing. Hawthorne suggests that Phoebe's love has transformed Holgrave, allowing hidden aspects of his self to be acknowledged and drawing him toward wholeness and community.[11]

Colonel Pyncheon, the ancestor responsible for the family curse, overshadows the entire novel. Although he has been dead for a long time, he still exerts a powerful influence over his descendants. Even his portrait seems ready to leave its frame in order to exert that influence. Throughout the story, reference is made to the colonel. Hepzibah, in particular, fears his power over her life and over the lives of the other members of the Pyncheon family. Still, when a suggestion is made to take down his portrait, she strongly protests.

THEMES

Perhaps the most important theme in *The House of the Seven Gables* is the effects of ancestral sin on future generations. Having read the Bible, Hawthorne was most likely acquainted with the passage that states, "The LORD is longsuffering and abundant in mercy, forgiving iniquity and transgression; but He by no means clears the guilty, visiting the iniquity of the fathers on the children to the third and fourth generation."[12] The greed that drives Colonel Pyncheon to play a part in the death of Matthew Maule is the sin that brings a curse on all future Pyncheons.

Isolation is another theme in *The House of the Seven Gables*. Each character is, in some way, isolated from the others and from society in general. Even Phoebe, in her exuberance, lives in a world of her own. Unlike the other characters, however, Phoebe overcomes her isolation through love.

The harm caused by isolation is evident particularly in the life of Hepzibah. In choosing to separate herself from humanity, she lives a dreary, desolate life. Phoebe, on the other hand, makes it a point to interact with people, whether in the cent shop or at church. This interaction with other human beings gives Phoebe life.

Although Clifford has been forcibly isolated most of his life, he comes alive only when he leaves the house and takes his famous train ride.[13] When Hepzibah asks him if what they are experiencing is a dream, Clifford replies with great gusto: "A dream,

Hepzibah!" repeated he, almost laughing in her face. "On the contrary, I have never been awake before!"[14]

Up until this point, Clifford had been isolated both in prison and in the house of the seven gables. As he journeys into the world of humanity, he experiences life. By the same token, only when Hepzibah interacts with her customers in the cent shop does she acquire the courage to stand up to Judge Jaffrey Pyncheon.

Another theme in *The House of the Seven Gables* is that of appearance vs. reality. This theme is most obvious in the characters of Hepzibah and Judge Jaffrey Pyncheon. Hepzibah, for example, *appears* to be evil because of the scowl on her face, but she is really kind and loyal. Judge Pyncheon *appears* to be kind and generous, but he is really a cold-hearted, greedy thief.

The theme of appearance vs. reality runs like a thread throughout the novel. For example, the ancestor, Colonel Pyncheon, was considered by the townspeople of his day to be a good and righteous man. In reality, however, he played a part in the killing of Matthew Maule, an innocent man.

Other themes in the novel include tradition vs. progress, upper class vs. working class, and heart vs. intellect. These themes are exemplified especially in the characters of Hepzibah, Phoebe, and Holgrave.

Hepzibah holds on to the trappings of a dying aristocracy, while Phoebe evokes the practicality of the simple humble class. Holgrave, on the other hand, represents the rise of the progressive middle class with its emphasis on scientific pursuits.

LITERARY DEVICES

The House of the Seven Gables is filled with symbolism. Among the symbols Hawthorne uses are the house itself, the elm tree, the tea set, the garden, the well in the garden, and Holgrave's daguerreotype. Each of these symbols adds depth and meaning to the story.

The most obvious symbol is the house itself. Its decay represents the decaying family that lives within its walls. The decay of the family is not only physical, but also, more importantly, moral and psychological. The house has become a prison in which Hepzibah and Clifford are inmates.

Outside the house stands the elm tree which, in contrast to the house, is flourishing at nearly one hundred years of age. Also outside the house is the garden, another symbol of growth and prosperity. It is interesting to note that, for the most part, life and love reign outside the house, whereas misery and death reign within it. Phoebe goes to the garden to meet Holgrave and to rest, and Clifford goes to the garden to enjoy the bees.

71

In employing these symbols, Hawthorne contrasts the worlds of light and darkness, heart and intellect, life and death. The interior of the house, which represents death, stands in stark contrast to the exterior, which represents life. Also, Hepzibah's dark mood contrasts sharply with Phoebe's lightheartedness.

This contrast of light and dark is especially significant in the symbol of the daguerreotype. The process of creating a daguerreotype involved the use of a mirrored plate that contained both a positive and a negative image. Michael Bunker observes:

> The importance of light in impressing the image onto the mirrored plate becomes crucial to understanding the metaphoric value of the daguerreotype for Hawthorne. . . . Just as the daguerreotype contains both a positive and a negative image, Holgrave believes it capable of containing both the light and dark of the soul.[15]

Hawthorne's masterful and penetrating depiction of both the light and dark aspects of the human soul has given *The House of the Seven Gables* a prominent place in American literature. Had Hawthorne written only this novel, his name as a great writer would be firmly established.

Faith and Sin

"Young Goodman Brown" and "The Minister's Black Veil"

Two of Hawthorne's best known short stories are "Young Goodman Brown" and "The Minister's Black Veil." In each of them, Hawthorne analyzes the problem of sin, particularly the sins of isolation and hypocrisy.

"Young Goodman Brown"

"Young Goodman Brown" first appeared in 1846 in a two-volume collection of stories entitled *Mosses from an Old Manse*. Seventeen of them were written at Hawthorne's home in Concord, Massachusetts, where he and Sophia moved shortly after their marriage. This home was called *The Manse* and was located near the bridge where the first shots of the Revolutionary War were fired. "Young Goodman Brown" would become one of Hawthorne's best known short stories.

PLOT DEVELOPMENT

"Young Goodman Brown" is the story of a young man married for only three months to a lovely young woman named Faith. The story opens with Goodman Brown leaving his house at sunset to go on a mysterious journey. He leaves against the wishes of his wife. Sensing that he is heading for danger, she begs him to stay home. But he refuses, stating that he must take his journey "'twixt now and sunrise."[1]

After he has gone a little way, Goodman Brown looks back and sees Faith watching him "with a melancholy air."[2] Goodman feels guilty at leaving his young bride. He promises that upon his return, he will "cling to her skirts and follow her to heaven."[3]

Goodman heads for the forest where he knows he will face the worst kind of evil. In the forest, he meets a middle-aged man holding a staff that looks like "a great black snake."[4] This man represents the devil himself. His staff represents the power the devil has over those who choose to follow him.

After Goodman Brown has walked a short distance into the forest, he has second thoughts. He suddenly remembers that he comes from a long line of Christians and that a Christian should not be walking with the devil.

My father never went into the woods on such an errand, nor his father before him. We have been a race of honest men and good Christians since the days of the martyrs; and shall I be the first of the name of Brown that ever took this path and kept—".

"Such company, thou wouldst say," observed the elder person, interrupting his pause.[5]

So Goodman Brown tells the devil that he intends to return home.

But the devil interrupts him with the shocking news that Brown's ancestors were not the Christians Brown thinks they were. On the contrary, they too chose to follow the devil. To make matters worse, the devil tells Goodman Brown that some of the people whom Brown now considers good Christians are really not.

As the devil reveals this distressing news, Goodman Brown's Sunday school teacher, Goody Cloyse, appears before him. Goodman is quite surprised to find her in the woods at this time of night. He hides so that she will not notice him walking with the devil.

As he listens to his Sunday school teacher's conversation with the devil, Goodman Brown is shocked to discover that she is really a witch. He also learns that she is on her way to the devil's communion table. When he then discovers that his pastor and a deacon of his church are also involved in devil worship, Brown's distress approaches its limits.

The worst shock of all occurs when Brown discovers that his very own wife, Faith, has turned to the devil. At this point, Brown plunges into despair and follows his wife to the diabolical communion ceremony. There, as he is about to be baptized into the devil's congregation, he cries out to Faith to look toward Heaven and save herself. Then, suddenly, Goodman Brown finds himself alone.

The next morning, he returns to Salem, a totally changed man. For the rest of his life, he never again trusts anyone and chooses to live separated from his family and friends.

"Young Goodman Brown" has been compared to Goethe's *Faust*. Faust, of course, sells his soul to the devil. Although Goodman Brown is never baptized into the devil's congregation, he chooses, nevertheless, to follow the path of evil that night. This choice affects him negatively for the rest of his life.

LITERARY DEVICES

"Young Goodman Brown" is rich in symbolism. Some of the key symbols found in the story include:

- *Goodman's wife, Faith*. Her name represents the faith that Goodman Brown betrays in choosing to follow the devil. Had he chosen to remain with

Faith instead of going on his journey, he would not have gotten into trouble.

- *Goodman Brown's own name.* He appears to be a "good man," but is made to wonder if anyone is truly good.

- *Faith's pink ribbons.* Pink is a blend of white and red. In making the ribbons pink, Hawthorne may have been saying that Faith, like all human beings, is a combination of innocence (white) and sin (red).

Another literary device used in this story is ambiguity. Hawthorne does not make clear whether Goodman Brown's journey actually took place or is only a dream. He leaves it up to the reader to decide. What *is* clear, however, is that Hawthorne wants to make his reader aware that sin exists in all people.

A key message in "Young Goodman Brown" is that even flirting with evil is dangerous. Had Goodman Brown not chosen to take his evil journey, he would not have suffered the consequences of it.

"THE MINISTER'S BLACK VEIL"

Like "Young Goodman Brown," "The Minister's Black Veil," first published in 1835, is an ambiguous story open to more than one interpretation.

PLOT DEVELOPMENT

"The Minister's Black Veil" tells the story of a thirty-year-old, highly respected pastor named Reverend Hooper. He is a kind and merciful man, with a special love for his congregation:

> Mr. Hooper had the reputation of a good preacher, but not an energetic one: he strove to win his people heavenward by mild, persuasive influences, rather than to drive them thither by the thunders of the Word.[6]

One Sunday, Reverend Hooper appears at church with a black veil hanging over his face, so low that it is "shaken by his breath."[7] The veil causes quite a stir among his congregation. Some believe that he "has changed himself into something awful."[8]

Others think he has gone crazy: "'Our parson has gone mad!' cried Goodman Gray, following him across the threshold."[9] Still others think he is hiding a terrible sin:

> A rumor of some unaccountable phenomenon had preceded Mr. Hooper into the meeting-house, and set all the congregation astir. . . . But that piece of crape, to their imagination, seemed to hang down before his heart, the symbol of a fearful secret between him and them.[10]

It is interesting to note that on the first day Reverend Hooper wears the black veil, he conducts the funeral of a young girl from his parish. Hawthorne implies that Reverend Hooper may have sinned with this young girl and that this is the reason he has begun to wear the veil.[11]

This assumption of sin on the minister's part is further supported by his sermon that Sunday. He preaches on secret sin, a message that creates considerable discomfort among his congregation. The reason for this discomfort is, as Hawthorne implies, the awareness that every person is guilty of secret sin. The minister's black veil serves as a mirror to this truth. The eyes have been called "the windows of the soul." When Mr. Hooper covers his eyes with the black veil, his parishioners are no longer able to look into his soul. Instead, they are forced to look into their own souls filled with sin. On the one hand, Mr. Hooper's black veil, then, is but a reflection of the invisible black veil that covers each person's own secret sin. On the other hand, it is what causes the minister to see "all with a darkened aspect."[12]

As the story progresses, several people try in vain to get Mr. Hooper to remove his black veil. Despite her persistent pleas, even Elizabeth, Reverend Hooper's fiancée, cannot get him to remove the veil. Consequently, she eventually breaks off their engagement.

THEMES

In choosing to isolate himself from Elizabeth, from his congregation, and from his community, Hooper personifies Hawthorne's recurring theme of isolation. This deliberate isolation causes Mr. Hooper to spend the rest of his life in lonely misery, separated from the relationships that would bring light to his life. Instead, he opts to remain isolated behind both a literal and a figurative black veil.

When he reaches the end of his life, Hooper still refuses to remove the veil. Instead, he holds it more tightly than ever against his face. This clinging to the veil very likely represents Hooper's clinging to the secret sin in his life. At this point, Hawthorne shows his reader what he believed was the real danger of secret sin:

> What, but the mystery which it obscurely typifies, has made this piece of crape so awful? When the friend shows his innermost heart to his friend; the lover to his best-beloved; when man does not vainly shrink from the eye of his Creator, loathsomely treasuring up the secret of his sin; then deem me a monster, for the symbol beneath which I have lived, and die! I look around me, and, lo! on every visage a Black veil.[13]

Critics have given various reasons for Reverend Hooper's decision to wear the black veil. Some believe that he wears it as a constant reminder that every person harbors his own secret sin. Other critics, however, present the view that Mr. Hooper is, indeed, guilty of his own secret sin. This latter view is more consistent with Hawthorne's other works. As we have already seen, the theme of secret sin permeates *The Scarlet Letter*, *The House of the Seven Gables*, and "Young Goodman Brown."

Regardless of Reverend Hooper's reason for wearing the black veil, it is a symbol of the isolation caused by sin. Mr. Hooper's secret sin destroys his relationship with his fiancée, with his congregation, and with his community.

At the end of the story the question remains: Why did Reverend Hooper don the black veil? Was it to hide some secret sin, or was it to reflect to others their own secret sin? The answer to this question is one that Hawthorne, with typical ambiguity, leaves up to his reader.

CRIMES AGAINST NATURE

"Rappaccini's Daughter" and "Ethan Brand"

"Rappaccini's Daughter" is one of Hawthorne's better known short stories. It is based on a true incident that happened during the author's lifetime.

In 1842, a scandal occurred surrounding a certain Dr. Robert Wesselhoeft of Boston. Dr. Wesselhoeft was accused by Dr. Oliver Wendell Holmes of being a quack. Wesselhoeft was a homeopathic physician who ran a spa in the village of West Roxbury, near Boston. This spa provided a supposed water cure for all kinds of diseases.

Homeopathic medicine was considered dangerous by the medical community of Hawthorne's day. Dr. Holmes gave two lectures entitled "Homeopathy and Its Kindred Delusions" in which he denounced Wesselhoeft and his fellow homeopaths. Holmes described Wesselhoeft as one of those "Empirics [quacks], ignorant barbers, and men of that sort . . . who announced themselves ready to relinquish all the accumulated treasure of our art, to trifle with life upon the strength of these fantastic theories."[1] As a result of Holmes's accusation, Wesselhoeft was forced to close his medical practice in Boston.

quack—*Someone who falsely claims to possess medical skill.*

When Holmes made his accusation about Wesselhoeft, Hawthorne was living in West Roxbury as part of the Brook Farm community. He undoubtedly heard of the incident, probably from Holmes himself, who was a friend of the author.

But Hawthorne also had a more personal connection with Dr. Wesselhoeft. The latter's younger brother, William Wesselhoeft, was likewise a physician who, interestingly, took care of Hawthorne's wife Sophia. Without Hawthorne's knowledge, William Wesselhoeft used hypnosis to treat Sophia, a practice that greatly angered Hawthorne. As Thomas St. John has observed, "An experiment in hypnotism was, to Hawthorne, an attempt to violate a woman's 'reserve and sanctity of soul,' an effort to reduce her to a 'performing beast on the stage.'"[2]

Moreover, Sophia's father, Dr. Nathaniel Peabody, was also a physician who embraced homeopathy. Against his better judgment, he treated Sophia's illnesses by prescribing excessive and powerful doses of homeopathic medicines that caused her to be in an almost continual state of lethargy.

Both of these experiences—his father-in-law's experimentation with Sophia and Dr. William Wesselhoeft's use of hypnotism—greatly upset Hawthorne. He took both the incident surrounding Holmes's accusation of Wesselhoeft and his own personal experiences surrounding his wife Sophia and, in 1844, fashioned them into the provocative short story entitled "Rappaccini's Daughter."

"RAPPACCINI'S DAUGHTER"

The story first appeared in 1846 in Hawthorne's collection of short stories entitled *Mosses from an Old Manse*. On the surface, it is about the rivalry that exists between two well-known scientists, Pietro Baglioni and Giacomo Rappaccini. In essence, however, the story deals with the dangers of science in the hands of people greedy for power.

Baglioni is highly respected in the scientific community, whereas Rappaccini is considered to be a quack. Although a traditional scientist, Baglioni secretly envies Rappaccini's success and wants to destroy him. At the same time, however, Baglioni is concerned about the horrors perpetrated by scientists with a lust to play God. Consequently, he strongly opposes Rappaccini's scientific methods, thus creating a rift between the two men.

Like "The Birthmark," "Rappaccini's Daughter" reveals Hawthorne's concern with the dangers of unrestrained scientific inquiry. Samuel Chase Coale describes this danger as "the psychology of idolatry."[3] Michael Colacurcio echoes this concern, describing unbridled scientific experimentation as:

> [R]esearch gone amok, rendered dangerous and unethical by virtue of the personal motives of the physician-scientist, his self-imposed isolation from his peers, and the unmonitored nature and progress of his project which inevitably results in the death of at least one innocent other.[4]

PLOT DEVELOPMENT

"Rappaccini's Daughter" takes place in Padua, Italy, during the sixteenth century. The story revolves around Beatrice Rappaccini, the beautiful and innocent daughter of the diabolical scientist, Giacomo Rappaccini. The name Beatrice means "blessed one." But far from being blessed, Beatrice has been cursed by her father's sorcery. Driven by his lust for power, Signor Rappaccini has kept Beatrice isolated from the world around her. She spends most of her lonely days tending to her father's garden.

Rappaccini has spent his life raising poisonous plants in this garden, in the hope of discovering superior medical knowledge. Motivated by pride, he will stop at nothing to gain this knowledge, not even his own daughter's well-being. He uses Beatrice as the object of his wicked experiments. In the process, she becomes so infected with poison that her very breath is filled with it. Whatever she touches or breathes on dies instantly.

Despite her horrible fate, Beatrice has one bright spot in her life. It is her love for the young scientist, Giovanni Guasconti. Giovanni takes up lodging next door to Rappaccini's poisonous garden. Giovanni spots Beatrice from his window and eventually falls in love with her.

Giovanni is the son of Signor Baglioni's close friend. Because of this relationship, Baglioni feels that he must protect Giovanni from Rappaccini's evil influence. Baglioni warns Giovanni against becoming involved with Beatrice or her father, claiming she is as "poisonous as she is beautiful."[5]

But Baglioni's warning comes too late. Giovanni has already been badly smitten by Beatrice's beauty. To his great horror, he too has become infected by the poisons in the garden. He discovers that a bouquet of flowers that he has purchased for Beatrice withers in his hand: "those dewy flowers were already beginning to droop; they wore the aspect of things that had been fresh and lovely yesterday."[6] Immediately thereafter, with the merest sigh of his breath he kills a spider that was spinning its web in his room.

Giovanni now faces a serious dilemma. If he stays with Beatrice in the garden, he too will kill everything he touches and everything he breathes on. In a fit of anguish and anger, Giovanni blames Beatrice for infecting him:

> "Yes, poisonous thing!" repeated Giovanni, beside himself with passion. "Thou hast done it! Thou hast blasted me! Thou hast filled my veins with poison! Thou hast made me as hateful, as ugly, as loathsome and deadly a creature as thyself—a world's wonder of hideous monstrosity!"[7]

Stunned by the realization that she has become a monster to Giovanni, Beatrice takes a medication developed by Baglioni as an antidote to her poisoned state. Instead of healing her, however, the medicine kills her. Hawthorne writes: "To Beatrice, . . . as poison had been life, so the powerful antidote was death."[8]

THEMES

Critics differ as to their final interpretation of "Rappaccini's Daughter." As Laura Stallman observes:

> There has been no general agreement as to the tale's interpretation and there is still no clear

emerging consensus yet regarding its meaning. It has aroused a bewildering array of conflicting interpretations. The tale's meaning has been construed to be pro-Transcendental and anti-Transcendental. Beatrice has been regarded as a heavenly angel and a fatal seductress. Giovanni has been characterized as a Puritan and an artist figure. Rappaccini has been deemed both God and Satan. And Baglioni has been seen as an ineffectual Christ and a Iago-like figure.[9]

Despite conflicting interpretations of "Rappaccini's Daughter," one thing is clear: blind devotion to science leads to tragedy. In conducting his experiments in isolation from the established scientific community, Rappaccini reveals that his is a search not for knowledge, but for power.

"ETHAN BRAND"

"Ethan Brand" is one of Hawthorne's most popular short stories, evoking some of his most vivid imagery. Few readers will forget Brand's climb to the top of the fiery kiln before throwing himself into it:

Ethan Brand stood erect, and raised his arms on high. The blue flames played upon his face, and imparted the wild and ghastly light which alone could have suited its expression; it was that of a fiend on the verge of plunging into his gulf of intensest torment.[10]

Unlike some of his other stories, Hawthorne had a difficult time writing "Ethan Brand": "I have wrenched and torn an idea out of my miserable brain, or rather, the fragment of an idea, like a tooth ill-drawn and leaving the roots to torture me."[11]

In calling his story "the fragment of an idea,"[12] Hawthorne implies that he probably originally intended this story to be a novel; hence, the subtitle "A Chapter from an Abortive Romance."

PLOT DEVELOPMENT

Ethan Brand is a lime-burner by trade near the town of North Adams, Massachusetts. He leaves his town and his trade to search for the Unpardonable Sin. According to Mark Harris, the unpardonable sin is "divorcing one's head from one's heart and oneself from humanity,"[13] a common theme throughout Hawthorne's work.

As the story begins, a man named Bartram is tending a kiln, the same kiln once tended by Ethan Brand. The kiln sits on a hill called Mount Graylock. With Bartram is his young son, Joe, a very sensitive boy. Joe hears strange laughter coming from the foot of Mount Graylock and becomes frightened: "But, father . . . he does not laugh like a man that is glad. So the noise frightens me!"[14]

The laughter comes from Ethan Brand, whose

approaching footsteps the young boy hears. Suddenly Brand appears. After a few words of conversation, Brand tells Bartram that he once tended the very same kiln that Bartram is now tending.

As Brand thinks back on his early days in that town, he remembers the man he once was—recalling the "tenderness [and] love and sympathy for mankind" that "became the inspiration of his life."[15]

But then, as Hawthorne points out, Ethan becomes a victim of the thinking of his day. This thinking "disturbed the counterpoise between his mind and heart."[16] The more knowledge Brand gained, the harder his heart became: "[Intellect] possessed his life. . . . But where was the heart? That, indeed, had withered, had contracted, had hardened, had perished! It had ceased to partake of the universal throb. He had lost his hold of the magnetic chain of humanity."[17]

This hardness of heart caused him to look on people as merely subjects of experimentation. Worst of all, for the purpose of his scientific studies, Brand influenced people to commit all kinds of crimes:

> [H]e was now a cold observer, looking on mankind as the subject of his experiment, and, at length, converting man and woman to be his puppets, and pulling the wires that moved them to such degrees of crime as were demanded for his study.[18]

THEMES

In the end, Ethan Brand discovers the Unpardonable Sin within his own heart. What is this unpardonable sin? Hawthorne implies that it is the sin of putting more value on the intellect than on the heart. Jerry Keen offers an interesting explanation:

> Perhaps, the unpardonable sin is a heart so calloused and depraved, that true heartfelt repentance . . . is beyond the realm of possibility. In the end, the unforgivable sin is not that it is so terrible that God cannot forgive, but that man's heart, like that of Ethan Brand, becomes so hard over time that he cannot repent.[19]

Paul Elmer More describes the Unpardonable Sin as "the sin of banishing from the breast all those natural, spontaneous emotions in the pursuit of an idea."[20] Like "Rappaccini's Daughter," "Ethan Brand" exposes the dangers of elevating the intellect above the heart. Ethan Brand does so and loses his humanness: "Thus Ethan Brand became a fiend."[21]

WAR OF THE HEART AND MIND

"The Birthmark," "The May-Pole of Merrymount," and "The Artist of the Beautiful"

Three lesser known stories by Hawthorne are "The Birthmark," "The May-Pole of Merry Mount," and "The Artist of the Beautiful." Each of these stories considers a central theme or concern of Hawthorne's fiction.

"THE BIRTHMARK"

"The Birthmark" is the story of a mad scientist named Aylmer and his beautiful wife Georgiana. Georgiana is physically perfect except for a small crimson birthmark on her left cheek. Hawthorne describes this birthmark in detail:

[I]n the centre of Georgiana's left cheek there was a singular mark, deeply interwoven, as it were, with the texture and substance of her face. In the usual state of her complexion—a healthy though delicate bloom—the mark wore a tint of deeper crimson, which imperfectly defined its shape amid the surrounding rosiness. When she blushed it gradually became more indistinct, and finally vanished amid the triumphant rush of blood that bathed the whole cheek with its brilliant glow. . . . Its shape bore not a little similarity to the human hand, though of the smallest pygmy size.[1]

PLOT DEVELOPMENT

Aylmer becomes so obsessed with this physical flaw on his wife's face that he determines to use his scientific power to remove it. His thoughts and actions reveal his evil heart and selfish motives. Instead of loving his wife for her character, he considers her a trophy that must be made perfect.

At first, Georgiana is deeply hurt by her husband's attitude toward the birthmark. He claims that it is keeping him from loving her. When Aylmer tells her that the birthmark shocks him, she cries out in anguish:

"Shocks you, my husband?" cried Georgiana, deeply hurt; at first reddening with momentary anger, but then bursting into tears. "Then why did you take me from my mother's side? You cannot love what shocks you!"[2]

Aylmer insists, however, that he can surgically remove the mark. He convinces Georgiana to become the subject of his scientific experimentation. She believes that it is the only way she can save her marriage. Moreover, she herself now finds the mark horrifying and wants to be rid of it.

In the secrecy of his laboratory, Aylmer prepares a potion that will permanently remove the birthmark. With the aid of his assistant, Aminadab, he concocts a poisonous drink and gives it to his wife. At first, success seems sure. But as the birthmark fades from Georgiana's cheek, so does the life fade from her body. Although Aylmer succeeds in removing the birthmark, he also succeeds in killing his wife.

THEMES

"The Birthmark" deals with the dangers of unbridled scientific inquiry, a recurring theme in Hawthorne's work. Aylmer has been compared to Frankenstein in Mary Shelley's novel by the same name. Like Frankenstein, Aylmer is deceived into thinking that his scientific experiments are for the good of humanity. In reality, however, he is a proud and selfish man filled with a lust for power.

In the character of Aylmer, Hawthorne reveals his

concern about his era's fascination with the power of science. Like those opposed to genetic engineering today, Hawthorne worried that scientists were seeking knowledge for the wrong reasons.

Commenting on "The Birthmark," Karen Bernardo writes:

> Aylmer is used to seeing the world, not as a miracle or wonder, but as a code waiting to be cracked, and he cannot see Georgiana's birthmark in any positive way. It mocks him because he is a scientist and she is his wife; he should be able to make her absolutely flawless.[3]

Aylmer chooses to be ruled by his head (the mad pursuit of scientific power). In the process, he loses his heart (his precious wife and her love).

Although Aylmer is evil, Georgiana is not a totally innocent victim. She fails to realize that her worth does not depend on her appearance. Instead, she allows herself to be influenced by her diabolical husband. This weakness in her character causes her to lose her life. Indeed, as the story ends, we realize that the flaw on Georgiana's heart is worse than the flaw on her face.

Far from being a mere superficial flaw, the birthmark represents Georgiana's union with humanity:

> It was the fatal flaw of humanity which Nature, in one shape or another, stamps ineffaceably on all

her productions, either to imply that they are temporary and finite, or that their perfection must be wrought by toil and pain.[4]

Like "Rappaccini's Daughter," "The Birthmark" warns of the horrible dangers that await the person who tries to play God. In attempting to remove the birthmark, Aylmer is guilty of intellectual pride and of selfishness. He assumes that just because he thinks the birthmark is evil, it is. Moreover, his actions reveal the superficial nature of his love for Georgiana. Thus, the reader is left wondering who is the greater victim in this story—Georgiana or Aylmer.

"THE MAY-POLE OF MERRYMOUNT"

Michael Colacurcio describes "The May-Pole of Merry Mount" as "one of Hawthorne's most richly learned and ironically manipulated stories."[5] Based on an actual event that took place in colonial America, "The May-Pole of Merry Mount" is an allegory that deals with "the fusion of politics and piety in the Puritan world."[6] In the spring of 1624, there came to the new world a man named Thomas Morton. Morton arrived aboard a ship called the *Unity* whose captain

allegory—*A story expressing a truth about life through the use of symbols.*

was named Wollaston. Wollaston was presumably a trader from western England who sought to establish himself in New England as a fur trader.

The ship landed in what is now Quincy Bay, Massachusetts. Together with Wollaston, Morton established a plantation located northwest of Plymouth and called it Mount Wollaston. Today the former Mount Wollaston is the site of Quincy, Massachusetts. The plantation was also called "Mare Mount" (from the Latin word "mare" meaning "sea") because of its view of the sea. As a result of the paganistic practices of its inhabitants, the plantation also acquired the name of "Merry Mount."

Because of his profligate lifestyle, Morton was not well-received by the Puritans. Indeed, he was eventually arrested by Miles Standish and charged with misconduct by the people of Plymouth. A detailed account of his inappropriate behavior is found in William Bradford's famous *Of Plymouth Plantation*.[7] Also, in an informative work entitled *New England's Memorial*, written in 1669 by Nathaniel Morton, we read the following about Thomas Morton:

> The said Morton became lord of misrule, and maintained, as it were a school of Atheism, and after they had got some goods into their hands, and got much by trading with the Indians, they spent it as vainly in quaffing and drinking both wine and strong liquors in great excess, as

some have reported, ten pounds' worth in a morning, setting up a maypole, drinking and dancing about it, and frisking about it like so many fairies, or furies rather, yea and worse practices, as if they had anew revived and celebrated the feast of the Roman goddess Flora, or the beastly practices of the mad Bacchanalians. The said Morton likewise, to shew his poetry, composed sundry rhymes and verses, some tending to lasciviousness, and others to the detraction and scandal of some persons' names, which he affixed to his idle or idol may-pole; they changed also the name of their place, and instead of calling it Mount Wollaston, they called it the Merry Mount, as if this jollity would have lasted always.[8]

According to research done by Colacurcio, Hawthorne undoubtedly had read this account of Thomas Morton and drew directly from it to describe the maypole:

This venerated emblem was a pine tree, which had preserved the slender grace of youth, while it equalled the loftiest height of the old wood monarchs. From its top streamed a silken banner, colored like the rainbow. Down nearly to the ground the pole was dressed with birchen boughs, and others of the liveliest green, and some with silvery leaves, fastened by ribbons that fluttered in fantastic knots of twenty different colors, but no sad ones. . . . the shaft of the Maypole was stained with the seven brilliant hues of the banner at its top. On the lowest green bough hung an abundant wreath of roses, some that had been gathered in the sunniest spots of the forest, and others, of still richer blush, which the colonists had reared from English seed.[9]

PLOT DEVELOPMENT

Dressed in animal-like costumes, the people of Merry Mount are dancing wildly around the maypole in celebration of the marriage of Edgar and Edith, Lord and Lady of the May. The festivities are suddenly interrupted by the intrusion of the highly respected Puritan leader, John Endicott, and his lieutenant Peter Palfrey, accompanied by several other heavily armed Puritans. Robert Gale describes the scene as follows:

> They [the Puritans] cut down the colorful Maypole, arrest Edgar and Edith and their humorously disguised cohorts, shoot their dancing bear, and thus break up Merry Mount.[10]

It is John Endicott who cuts down the Maypole with his sword:

> And with his keen sword Endicott assaulted the hallowed Maypole. Nor long did it resist his arm. It groaned with a dismal sound; it showered leaves and rosebuds upon the remorseless enthusiast; and finally, with all its green boughs and ribbons

and flowers, symbolic of departed pleasures, down fell the banner staff of Merry Mount.[11]

THEMES

On a socio-political level, this cutting down of the maypole by the Puritans symbolizes their victory in early America. Endicott's closing words reveal this triumph: "Nor think ye, young ones, that they are the happiest, even in our lifetime of a moment, who mis-spend it in dancing round a Maypole!"[12] Also a sign of Puritan victory is the couple's growth from irre-sponsibility to responsibility, ethical responsibility being a major tenet of Puritan thought.

On a psychological level, the cutting down of the Maypole represents the essential conflict between the joy of nature and the gloom of the law, a conflict seemingly resolved during the Romantic era. As Colacurcio observes, "The May-Pole of Merry Mount" deals with "the relation between original Puritanism and 'the future complexion of New England.'"[13]

fable—*A supernatural story in which animals often speak and act like human beings; a story intended to present a uni-versal truth.*

"The May-Pole of Merry Mount" has the characteristics of a fable. Although there are no strong characters in the story, it leaves the reader with a strong message. That message is that neither the extreme of Puritanical rigidity nor the extreme of Mortonian excess will bring freedom. According to Donald Conners, Hawthorne's message in "The May-Pole of Merry Mount" is that happiness is found only "in balanced and moderate living."[14]

"THE ARTIST OF THE BEAUTIFUL"

"The Artist of the Beautiful" is a story about a watchmaker named Owen Warland. Owen has a gift for working with small objects. Hawthorne describes him as possessing a "microscopic" mind that "tended naturally to the minute."[15]

PLOT DEVELOPMENT

Owen has a dream to create a small machine filled with life. Like many artists, however, he is misunderstood—and even ridiculed—by the people in his life. One such person is Peter Hovenden. Owen formerly worked for Hovenden as an apprentice in his watch shop. Another person who does not understand Owen is his former classmate, Robert Danforth. Danforth is a practical blacksmith who plies his trade with no concept of creative beauty. Only Annie, Peter Hovenden's daughter, seems to understand Owen. In the end, however, she too fails to grasp the meaning of Owen's search and ends up marrying Danforth.

Despite many obstacles, Owen pursues and finally achieves his dream of creating a life-like, mechanical butterfly. One day, Owen visits Annie and Danforth, who now have a child. Owen brings the mechanical butterfly as a wedding gift for the young couple. When he opens the ebony box to release the butterfly, Annie is startled and "almost screamed as a butterfly fluttered forth."[16]

Observing the butterfly with delight, Annie asks if it is alive or if Owen created it. Her husband, some-what sarcastically, says that it is alive. But it is Owen who answers Annie's question:

> "Alive? Yes, Annie; it may well be said to possess life, for it has absorbed my own being into itself. . . . Yes; I created it. But"—and here his counte-nance somewhat changed—"this butterfly is not now to be what it was when I beheld it afar off in the daydreams of my youth."[17]

Owen's words almost seem like a prediction of what happens next. At Danforth's request, Annie passes the butterfly to her husband's fingers. From there, the butterfly begins to flutter around the room again. Annie's baby spots the brilliant creature. After a few more flights among the adults, the butterfly approaches the baby. The baby snatches it and crushes it in his hand.

Instead of being crushed himself, Owen looks peacefully at the crushed butterfly:

> And as for Owen Warland, he looked placidly at what seemed the ruin of his life's labor, and which was yet no ruin. He had caught a far other butterfly than this.[18]

Owen realizes that what matters most is not that he has created the butterfly, but that he has accomplished his dream.

THEMES

In this tale, the question of the artist's ambivalence is significant. Because of the Puritan influence in his life, Hawthorne was torn between the danger of misuing the imagination and the artistic imperative of yielding to it.

Like Owen, Hawthorne also struggled to be understood by the society in which he created. Millicent Bell describes "The Artist of the Beautiful" as "a melancholy defense of the life of art"[19] and states that this tale "represents Hawthorne's most sympathetic treatment of the idealistic view of artistic creation."[20]

According to Bell, Hawthorne expresses in this

tale his belief that the artist is "incapable of communicating the eternal truths apprehended in his lonely ecstasies."[21]

He alone must reconcile the dichotomy that exists within him between the practical and the ideal, the material and the spiritual, the intellect and the heart. Owen reconciles this dichotomy when he transcends matter as the butterfly flies from his hands. Bell observes:

> [W]ith the flight of the butterfly from its maker's hands, Owen's idealism has reached its highest level. He no longer expects to spiritualize matter; . . . he has transcended matter altogether.[22]

As Randall Clack notes, "Owen Warland, in 'The Artist of the Beautiful' . . . embodies Hawthorne's vision of the soul transformed by love."[23]

Undoubtedly, Hawthorne himself experienced misunderstanding at the hands of some of his contemporaries. Yet, at the same time, he greatly enjoyed his creative gift despite public criticism. In the end, Hawthorne, like Owen, eventually fulfilled his creative dreams, and the world is far richer as a result.

OLD AND NEW WORLDS

Examining **The Marble Faun** and *Selected Short Stories*

*T*he Marble Faun appeared in 1860. It is the last novel that Hawthorne finished before he died. Millicent Bell calls it his "pioneering 'international novel'"[1] not only because it takes place outside the United States, but also because it tells of the encounter of the Americans Kenyon and Hilda with the morality and culture of the Old World:

> Like [Henry] James's travelers later, Hawthorne's visitors to Rome find themselves putting their Americanness to the test. Sin and suffering overtake the European Miriam and Donatello, and in coming to terms with them the Americans undergo a trial of their inherited Puritan ethic.[2]

The novel was published at the same time both in England and in America. Its English title was *Transformation*, but its American title was *The Marble*

Faun. Hawthorne started writing the book in Rome, Italy, during the winter of 1859. Of all his romances, he thought *The Marble Faun* was his best work, although most critics disagree.

THE MARBLE FAUN

The setting of the book is in Rome. There are four main characters: Hilda, Miriam, Donatello, and Kenyon. Three of the characters—Miriam, Hilda, and Kenyon—are artists and Americans. Donatello is a young Italian count who looks like a faun. The title of the book takes its name from a statue of a faun by the famous Greek sculptor Praxiteles.

faun—*A creature of Roman mythology having the legs, hooves, and horns of a goat and the torso and head of a man.*

PLOT DEVELOPMENT

The story occurs against the political backdrop of Italy in the mid-1800s, when Rome was occupied by Napoleon III and ruled by the dictatorial Pope Pius IX. It was a time of great social and cultural upheaval. As the story unfolds, Donatello and the three artists meet in Rome. Donatello falls in love with Miriam. Unknown to Donatello and her friends, however, Miriam has a dark, mysterious past: "Miriam, fair as she looked, was plucked up out of a mystery, and had its roots still clinging to her."[3]

During the story, a strange phantom-like character appears who begins to stalk Miriam. Miriam has a mysterious and sinister connection with this stalker. One night, when the stalker approaches Miriam, Donatello kills him. Secretly, Miriam approves of this murder. As a result, the relationship between Miriam and Donatello becomes "cemented by blood."[4]

The murder has an effect not only on Donatello and Miriam, but also on Hilda and Kenyon. Hilda, who has witnessed the murder, appears to lose some of her purity as a result. Kenyon, although attracted to Miriam, eventually retreats from her.

The story centers around Miriam. Although she appears to be happy, she is deeply tormented. As with Hawthorne's other characters, Miriam represents the contrast between appearance and reality. To Donatello and her friends, she appears to be blameless but is really evil.

Augustus Kolich has called Miriam "one of Hawthorne's most politically active women,"[5] a woman "unique among Hawthorne's feminine protagonists."[6] Kolich notes that:

> Miriam consistently displays the courage and shrewdness to do what is necessary to remain alive and free, and her amazing ability to function within the dangerous politics of the Roman theocracy—particularly as a woman who may be Jewish—is obviously one reason why many readers,

especially contemporary ones, have wanted to know more about her.[7]

THEMES

In *The Marble Faun*, Hawthorne also expresses the conflict between the Old World (Europe) and the New World (America). The novel includes many references to the great art of Italy. In fact, many people of Hawthorne's day who read *The Marble Faun* used it as a guidebook on visits to Italy and its museums. Millicent Bell observes that "modern critics have usually been dismissive of the work's travelogue aspect."[8]

Of the four primary characters in the novel, Donatello is perhaps the most compelling. James Russell Lowell describes him as follows:

Nothing could be more original or imaginative than the conception of the character of Donatello in Mr. Hawthorne's new romance. His likeness to the lovely statue of Praxiteles, his happy animal temperament, and the dim legend of his pedigree are combined with wonderful art to reconcile us to the notion of a Greek myth embodied in an Italian of the nineteenth century; and when at length a soul is created in this primeval pagan, this child of earth, this creature of mere instinct, awakened through sin to a conception of the necessity of atonement, we feel, that, while we looked to be entertained with the airiest of fictions, we were dealing with the most august truths of psychology, with the most pregnant facts of modern history, and studying a profound parable of the development of the Christian Idea.[9]

The "Christian Idea" to which Lowell alludes is the idea that sin alienates and isolates man from God, from humanity, and from himself. Indeed, according to Richard Mezo, "The most important theme of *The Marble Faun* is the consideration of the consequences of man's alienation from other men, from God, and from nature."[10]

Emily Schiller also refers to this "Christian Idea" in describing the story's dominant themes as "sin, suffering, and forgiveness."[11]

The Marble Faun is one of Hawthorne's deepest novels. Like most of his other works, it reveals the dichotomy between the intellect and the heart. This dichotomy is most clearly represented in the two pairs of characters: Kenyon and Hilda who represent the intellect, and Donatello and Miriam who represent the heart. Richard Mezo writes: "In *The Marble Faun*, Hawthorne is not presenting solutions as much as he is presenting choices. Donatello and Miriam incline to the way of the heart; Kenyon and Hilda to the way of the head."[12]

parable—*A short story that illustrates a moral attitude or a spiritual principle.*

The Marble Faun is, perhaps, one of Hawthorne's

109

most misunderstood works, lending itself to different and sometimes opposite interpretations. Despite such misunderstanding, however, it remains a tribute to the literary genius of one of America's greatest authors.

THE BLITHEDALE ROMANCE

In *The Blithedale Romance*, Hawthorne tells about his "experiences and observations at Brook Farm."[13] This novel was published in 1852. As we learned earlier, Brook Farm was a place in Massachusetts where a group of people called Transcendentalists tried to establish the perfect society. Although Hawthorne spent a few months at Brook Farm, his heart was never fully into the experience. It appears that he had "little interest in ideas or ideology; his subject as always was the family and human dysfunctioning."[14] In other words, Hawthorne was not primarily a man of ideas. He was a man of relationships. Because he realized the flaws in human nature, he could not accept the Transcendentalist belief in a perfect world where everyone would love one another. Hawthorne was too much of a realist to be influenced by such an idealistic view.

PLOT DEVELOPMENT

Four main characters fill the pages of *The Blithedale Romance* and provide the focus of the story. They are Zenobia, her half-sister Priscilla, Hollingsworth, and Miles Coverdale. All four of these characters are disillusioned with the progress of society and seek to escape it. As the story reveals, however, they are not really trying to escape society. They are trying to escape personal family problems. By coming to Blithedale, they attempt to set up an experiment in living that will restore them to the original Garden of Eden where there were no problems.

But Blithedale does not eliminate problems; it exposes them in a way that provides the central drama of the story.

Miller remarks that Zenobia, Priscilla, Hollingsworth, and Coverdale came to Blithedale "not to give but to receive."[15] This selfish attitude is what causes their personal failure and the failure of the Blithedale experiment.

THEMES

As the story unfolds, the reader learns that Zenobia and Priscilla are half-sisters and daughters of the same father. Zenobia grew up in wealth and luxury, while Priscilla grew up in poverty. Zenobia is a strong-willed feminist whose character is based on

Hawthorne's strong-willed feminist Margaret Fuller. Priscilla, on the other hand, is quiet and submissive. Other than their father, the common thread in both of their lives is a man named Hollingsworth. Although Hollingsworth appears to be a philanthropist, he really wants Zenobia's wealth. Although Zenobia falls in love with Hollingsworth, he eventually marries the submissive Priscilla. In the end, full of despair, Zenobia kills herself.

What started out as a promising experiment in living ends up a tragedy. Although Zenobia, Priscilla, Hollingsworth, and Coverdale go to Blithedale looking for a problem-free life, they discover that their problems are really inside themselves.

"THE CELESTIAL RAIL-ROAD"

"The Celestial Rail-road " first appeared in 1843 in a collection called *Twice-Told Tales*. Strongly influenced by Paul Bunyan's *Pilgrim's Progress*, it is an allegory that borders on fantasy. Brian Attebery writes: "'The Celestial Rail-road' is a satire on modern philosophies, reviving with some wit the setting of Bunyan's *Pilgrim's Progress*, and, like it, continually trying to break out of the limits of allegory into independent fantasy."[16]

PLOT DEVELOPMENT

The story deals with a common temptation to think that there is an easy road to Heaven. The main character of the story boards the train to the Celestial City, another name for Heaven. Along the way, he encounters many temptations that threaten to keep him from reaching his destination. After many adventures, he reaches a river on the other side of which lies the Celestial City. A ferryboat is docked at the edge of this river, and people are boarding it.

fantasy—*A creation of the imagination including bizarre or grotesque characters and settings and often featuring surreal (unnatural or dream-like) events.*

The main character assumes that the ferryboat will take him across the river to the Celestial City. This assumption is a major part of the story's satire. Hubert Hoeltje notes:

> Sometimes man has deluded himself into believing that his imperfections, which he has indeed recognized, can be overcome with no great trouble. With what calm but withering satire, in "The Celestial Rail-road," are the passengers represented as taking their ease, on their journey to the Celestial City, in a modern railway train! How convenient has charity been made

satire—*A literary style in which human behaviors or institutions are held up for ridicule, often through the use of exaggeration, clever humor, and irony.*

113

by modern methods—through the manufacture of an individual morality by throwing the individual's quota of virtue into the common stock, and letting the president and directors take care that the aggregate amount is well applied! How different are these modern improvements from the case of poor Christian, in *Pilgrim's Progress*, who had to carry his heavy burden on his own back![17]

Mark Hanley also notes the satirical discrepancy between Bunyan's classic and Hawthorne's work:

Hawthorne's modern travelers are undaunted by the trials that afflicted the pilgrims of John Bunyan's seventeenth-century tale. They surmount the "Slough of Despond" on a bridge of "French philosophy and German rationalism," sermons of "modern clergymen," and "books of morality." Though "Pope" and "Pagan" threatened Bunyan's voyagers in the Valley of the Shadow of Death, Hawthorne's rail passengers confront "a German by birth . . . called Giant Transcendentalist," a creature given to "strange phraseology" and shrouded by "fog and duskiness." His "capitalistic" Vanity Fair strikes his modern wayfarers as the "true and only heaven." They brand "piety" and "charity" as "useless anachronisms."[18]

When, however, the main character realizes with horror that the ferryboat is on its way to Hell, he tries to jump ship. A splash of cold water overtakes him and startles him back to his senses. With great relief, he realizes that his entire journey has been nothing more than a dream:

> I rushed to the side of the boat, intending to fling myself on shore; but the wheels, as they began their revolutions, threw a dash of spray over me so cold—so deadly cold, with the chill that will never leave those waters until Death be drowned in his own river—that with a shiver and a heartquake I awoke. Thank Heaven it was a Dream![19]

THEMES

According to Jonathan Cook, in "The Celestial Railroad," Hawthorne has "synthesized narrative or verse satire with apocalyptic, allegorical 'dream' vision."[20] Hawthorne used this synthesis to create a work that aptly reflects the age in which he lived, an age characterized by the tension between tradition and progress.

One sign of this transition was the invention of the railroad, which marked a turning point in the industrialization of America. The train symbolized freedom from the old way of doing business. It also symbolized personal freedom and prosperity. At the same time, the railroad brought with it many problems. One of these was greed, a problem that, as Hawthorne realized, often comes with increased prosperity. The travelers on the train are more concerned with the here-and-now than with their eternal destiny. As a result, they end up losing the blessings of eternal life. Only the two poor pilgrims, mocked and persecuted by the worldly-minded, eventually reach the shores of the Celestial City. There they are warmly welcomed and experience the joys of living forever with God.

The theme of sin and its consequences lies at the core of this short story. "The Celestial Rail-road" reflects Hawthorne's acquaintance with the Christian belief of a Heaven and a Hell. It also reflects his understanding that each person chooses whether he will go to Heaven or Hell. Although not one of his best known stories, "The Celestial Rail-road" is one of his most interesting and personally revealing.

"My Kinsman, Major Molineux"

"My Kinsman, Major Molineux" was first published in 1832. It was later included in a volume entitled *The Snow Image*. The story takes place a few years before the American Revolution. Knowing this is important to understanding the story. Hawthorne writes:

> The annals of Massachusetts Bay will inform us, that of six governors in the space of about forty years from the surrender of the old charter, under

James II, two were imprisoned by a popular insur-
rection; a third, as Hutchinson's history inclines to
believe, was driven from the province by the
whizzing of a musket-ball; a fourth, in the opinion
of the same historian, was hastened to his grave
by continual bickerings with the House of
Representatives; and the remaining two, as well as
their successors, till the Revolution, were favored
with few and brief intervals of peaceful sway.[21]

"My Kinsman, Major Molineux" is a commentary
on the fate of Thomas Hutchinson, the eighteenth-
century governor of Massachusetts. In 1765, as a
result of the Stamp Act protests, Governor
Hutchinson's home was destroyed by a mob much
like the one in "Major Molineux." Peter Shaw notes:

> The parallel with Hutchinson links the 1730s,
> when the story takes place, to the Revolutionary
> period that it is meant to evoke. Besides
> Hutchinson, other royal officials, as Hawthorne
> points out in the opening paragraph, suffered
> from mobs throughout the eighteenth century
> "until the Revolution." This observation permits
> the reader to view the mob that besets Major
> Molineux as a proto-Revolutionary one. But at the
> same time it establishes a complicated irony, for
> the information about the early mobs, Hawthorne
> also informs us, comes from "Hutchinson's
> History."[22]

PLOT DEVELOPMENT

The main character of the story is a young man named Robin. As the story opens, Robin is on a ferryboat headed to a town that is part of the Massachusetts Bay Colony. He has left the countryside to look for his relative, Major Molineux, a Colonial governor sent from England. Robin hopes that his relative will help him get started in a career.

Robin searches everywhere for his relative. Whenever he asks passersby if they know Major Molineux, some laugh and some get angry. But nobody gives Robin information about his kinsman.

Hawthorne, however, gives his reader an important clue as to what has happened to Major Molineux. This clue is the smell of tar as Robin enters the town:

> He now became entangled in a succession of crooked and narrow streets, which crossed each other, and meandered at no great distance from the water-side. The smell of tar was obvious to his nostrils, the masts of vessels pierced the moon-light above the tops of the buildings, and the numerous signs, which Robin paused to read, informed him that he was near the centre of business. But the streets were empty, the shops were closed, and lights were visible only in the second stories of a few dwelling-houses.[23]

Robin, of course, does not realize that Major Molineux is hated by the townspeople because he represents British rule in the colonies. Later in the story, however, when Robin learns that his relative has been tarred and feathered, he is shocked by the news: "His knees shook and his hair bristled with a mixture of pity and terror."[24] Now it is clear why people responded to Robin's questions as they did.

The story could be said to have two concurrent plots, involving two groups of people, both of which persecuted Thomas Hutchinson. As Shaw points out:

> On the one hand there was the Stamp Act crowd, which made Hutchinson a political scapegoat in the manner of the Molineux crowd. On the other hand there was the seemingly unprovoked treatment of Hutchinson by the patriot leaders, which is similar to that accorded Major Molineux by his nephew, Robin. Not the least of Hutchinson's ordeal lay in being accused of having hatched the Stamp Act when actually he had opposed it from the beginning. The crowd's refusal to recognize his innocence is not so surprising. But the fact that Hutchinson's fellow lawyers and legislators among the patriot opposition joined the crowd in identifying him with the Stamp Act is as surprising as Robin's joining the laughter of the mob when he first sees his suffering kinsman.[25]

Robin's failure to come to the aid of his relative seems surprising. Yet his behavior is required by

Hawthorne's purpose. Peter Shaw provides an explanation:

> Major Molineux represents authority. He is chosen as a scapegoat both by the crowd that is revolting from political authority and by his nephew, Robin. This young man, as psychoanalytic critics have shown, enacts the personal revolt against authority that is part of coming of age. When he joins with the crowd in ridiculing his uncle he is making him the scapegoat of his natural resentment at parental authority.[26]

Despite Robin's initial reaction to the plight of his uncle, he eventually feels remorse for his unkind behavior. Robin thinks that he should probably leave town because his kinsman "will scarce desire to see my face again."[27] But a kindly stranger encourages Robin not to leave, assuring him that he can make it on his own: "If you prefer to remain with us, . . . you may rise in the World without the help of your kinsman, Major Molineux."[28] The function of this stranger, according to Mary Jo Bona, is to help Robin "adjust to a new society. In effect, Robin is encouraged to forget his past in order to survive in a world that is indifferent to a commitment and a desire to remain with the family. His failure to adjust to the demands of a new culture may result in pain, violence, or even death."[29]

What Robin finally decides to do is unclear. But one thing is clear: Robin will make it on his own.

THEMES AND LITERARY DEVICES

The ending of "Major Molineux" differs somewhat from Hawthorne's other stories in that the reader is left with a sense of hope. John Gerlach observes that in most of his short stories, "Hawthorne creates the illusion of an open ending but in effect predicts that the outcome will be . . . a death in life. 'My Kinsman, Major Molineux' is a significant exception to this pattern."[30]

In "Major Molineux" the reader feels that, despite the uncertainty, the outcome will be a positive one. Gerlach also points out that:

Nineteenth-century stories that end on a note of uncertainty do, to be sure, exist: witness Hawthorne's "My Kinsman, Major Molineux." After Robin's ambiguous outburst of laughter directed at his kinsman during the symbolic parricide of tar and feathers, celebrated by onlookers with "counterfeited pomp, in senseless uproar, in frenzied merriment, trampling all on an old man's heart" (11:230), Hawthorne adds a touch that opens up the story. Robin wants to go home, to leave town to return to his village—"Will you

121

show me the way to the ferry?" (p. 231) he repeats—but the gentleman with him defers showing him, suggesting to Robin that he rise in the world without the help of his kinsman. We never learn whether Robin chooses his own village and consequently stagnation or an urban American destiny ambiguously short on decorum and stability.[31]

Like Hawthorne's other stories, this one is filled with symbolism. On one level, the story reflects the break between England and America at the time of the Revolutionary War. Major Molineux, an Englishman, represents England, the old country with its old way of doing things. Robin represents America, the young country, with its adventurous spirit and its desire for freedom. On another level, the story presents the psychological complexities inherent in a youth's coming of age as well as in a country's coming of age. Stephen Portch observes that "Hawthorne makes demands of his readers. The deliberate ambiguity he frequently employs—especially at the end of stories—requires the collaboration of sensitive readers. For Hawthorne does provide clues."[32]

It is the placement and discovery of these clues that makes "My Kinsman, Major Molineux" a provocative and pivotal story in Hawthorne's literary repertoire.

CLOSING THE CIRCLE

The Final Years and Enduring Legacy of Nathaniel Hawthorne

In addition to those works already discussed, Hawthorne wrote many others. Although most of them are not well-known today, they were popular in Hawthorne's time. Among these are his several collections of stories for children. These collections include *Grandfather's Chair* (1841), *A Wonder Book for Girls and Boys* (1852), and *Tanglewood Tales* (1853).

The stories in *A Wonder Book for Girls and Boys* and *Tanglewood Tales* are often based on Greek and Roman mythology. For example, three of the seven stories in the *Tanglewood Tales* are entitled "The Minotaur," "Circe's Palace," and "The Golden Fleece." The stories in *A Wonder Book for Girls and Boys* tell about King Midas, Medusa, Hercules, and Pandora. The book also includes stories about other mythological creatures that lived on fabled Mount Olympus. Two of the well-known stories in *A Wonder Book for Girls and Boys* are "The Three Golden Apples" and "The Gorgon's Head."

Both *Tanglewood Tales* and *A Wonder Book for Girls and Boys* are filled with lots of adventure. For this reason, they have been popular with children ever since they were first published.

GRANDFATHER'S CHAIR

In 1841, Hawthorne published his well-known collection of children's stories entitled *Grandfather's Chair*. This is one of the most delightful of his children's books. The stories in this collection tell about the history of the United States from the time of the Pilgrims until the Revolutionary War. They cover the period from 1620 to 1808. In his famous *Preface*, Hawthorne explains his purpose for writing this book:

> In writing this ponderous tome, the author's desire has been to describe the eminent characters and remarkable events of our annals in such a form and style that the YOUNG may make acquaintance with them of their own accord. For this purpose, while ostensibly relating the adventures of a chair, he has endeavored to keep a distinct and unbroken thread of authentic history.

The chair is made to pass from one to another of those personages of whom he thought it most desirable for the young reader to have vivid and familiar ideas, and whose lives and actions would best enable him to give picturesque sketches of the times.[1]

Hawthorne's preference for American history of the Colonial and Revolutionary periods is obvious in *Grandfather's Chair*. As Arlin Turner points out:

In biography and history Hawthorne evidenced his customary partiality for America of the Colonial and Revolutionary periods, and so included a preponderance of notes on figures, events, and monuments related to early New England. In the biographies his method was much the same as in the sketches that make up *Grandfather's Chair*: his custom was to choose one episode from the life of his subject and to elaborate on it, passing briefly over the remaining incidents.[2]

One could say that the main character in the book is Grandfather's chair. It is an old, oaken chair with a rich history. Hawthorne describes the physical appearance of the chair:

Now, the chair in which Grandfather sat was made of oak, which had grown dark with age, but had been rubbed and polished till it shone as bright as mahogany. It was very large and heavy, and had a back that rose high above Grandfather's white head. . . . On the very tip-top of the chair, over the head of Grandfather himself, was a likeness of a lion's head, which had such a savage grin that you would almost expect to hear it growl and snarl.[3]

As Grandfather's chair is moved from England to the New World, it passes from one owner to another. Among these owners are several historical figures, including Thomas Hutchinson, Cotton Mather, and George Washington. In a delightful way, Hawthorne brings these people to life. In the process, his readers learn important facts about the history of America. They also learn important lessons about life.

Hawthorne also brings the chair to life. In so doing, he uses the literary device of personification. In the memorable passage in Part III, Chapter 11, entitled "Grandfather's Dream," Grandfather and the chair engage in an enlightening conversation:

"And now, venerable chair, I have a favor to solicit. During an existence of more than two centuries you have had a familiar intercourse with men who were esteemed the wisest of their day. . . . Tell us, poor mortals, then, how we may be happy."

personification—*A literary device in which human characteristics are attributed to something that is not human.*

The lion's head [on top of the chair] fixed its eyes thoughtfully upon the fire. . . . as if it had a very important secret to communicate.

"As long as I have stood in

the midst of human affairs," said the chair, with a very oracular enunciation, "I have constantly observed that Justice, Truth, and Love are the chief ingredients of every happy life."[4]

After Hawthorne wrote *Grandfather's Chair*, he went to Brook Farm for about six months. There, as we have seen, he participated in the experiment in communal living about which he wrote in *The Blithedale Romance*. When he returned from Brook Farm, he wrote another series of children's stories. This series was called *True Stories* and was published in 1842. Like *Grandfather's Chair*, *True Stories* was about the lives of well-known people in history.

The following year, Hawthorne wrote a charming allegory for children called *Little Daffydowndilly*. In this story, the author teaches children about the Puritan work ethic. The main character, a spoiled little boy named Daffydowndilly, is sent by his mother to study with a stern schoolmaster named Mr. Toil. Daffydowndilly intensely dislikes Mr. Toil. Because of this, Daffydowndilly decides to run away from the school.

On the way, he meets an old man who also wants to flee from Mr. Toil. The two embark on a journey where they meet haymakers, carpenters, soldiers, and musicians. In every group, however, Daffydowndilly recognizes the face of Mr. Toil.

Frightened and upset, he continues to run away. To his surprise, he eventually realizes that his companion also looks like Mr. Toil. After a trip that has taken him in a big circle, Daffydowndilly comes to understand that Mr. Toil is not so bad after all. The story ends with the little boy's return to school, much wiser and more mature than when he left.

HAWTHORNE'S NOTEBOOKS

In addition to his fiction, Hawthorne also kept several notebooks throughout his life. Published after his death, these *Notebooks* contain valuable information about Hawthorne's life and thoughts. The *Notebooks* are divided into three groups: *The American Notebooks* (1868), *The English Notebooks* (1830), and *The French and Italian Notebooks* (1871).

A brief excerpt from *The English Notebooks* reveals Hawthorne's sensitivity to his surroundings as he walks the streets of London:

December 6, 1857

I have walked the streets a great deal in the dull November days, and always take a certain pleasure in being in the midst of human life,—as closely encompassed by it as it is possible to be anywhere in this world; and in that way of viewing it there is a dull and sombre enjoyment always to be had in Holborn, Fleet Street, Cheapside, and the other busiest parts of London. It is human life; it is this material world; it is a grim and heavy reality. I have never had the same sense of being surrounded by materialisms and hemmed in with the grossness of this earthly existence anywhere else; these broad, crowded streets are so evidently the veins and arteries of an enormous city. . . . [I]t is really an ungladdened life to wander through these huge, thronged ways, over a pavement foul with mud, ground into it by a million of footsteps; jostling against people who do not seem to be individuals, but all one mass. . . . [And] everywhere the dingy brick edifices heaving themselves up, and shutting out all but a strip of sullen cloud,that serves London for a sky.[5]

This passage is a prime example of Hawthorne's attention to details—details that, he hoped, would serve him well in future stories. As Edwards Hutchins Davidson observes in *Hawthorne's Last Phase*:

He knew, moreover, that a careful delineation of the landscape, of the architecture of English villages, and of anecdotes pertaining to odd, out-of-the-way burroughs would be of special help to him in the composition of a future romance. A ghost story about an old castle, a tree with a hollow trunk, an immense spider in the British Museum, a beautifully preserved asylum dating from Queen Elizabeth's day—these were the staple of his interest which assumed far greater space in the notebook than did any of the foreign policies of English and American diplomats. . . . To watch the patient storing of many insignificant details is to find the groundwork which Hawthorne laid for the romances of the last phase.[6]

In another delightful excerpt from *The American Notebooks*, Hawthorne tells of a canoe he purchased from his friend, Henry David Thoreau:

Sept. 2d. [1842] Friday.

Yesterday afternoon, while my wife, and Louisa, and I, were gathering the windfallen apples in our orchard, Mr. Thorow arrived with the boat. The adjacent meadow being overflowed by the rise of the stream, he had rowed directly to the foot of the orchard, and landed at the boards, after floating over forty or fifty yards of water, where people were making hay, a week or two since. I entered the boat with him, in order to have the benefit of a lesson in rowing and paddling. My little wife, who was looking on, cannot feel very proud of her husband's proficiency. I managed, indeed, to propel the boat by rowing with two oars; but the use of the single paddle is quite beyond my present skill. Mr. Thorow had assured me that it was only necessary to will the boat to go in any particular direction, and she would immediately take that course, as if imbued with the spirit of the steersman. It may be so with him, but certainly not with me; the boat . . . turned its head to every point of the compass except the right one. He then took the paddle himself, and though I could observe nothing peculiar in his management of it, the Musketaquid immediately became as docile as a trained steed. I suspect that she has not yet transferred her affections from her old master to her new one.[7]

In the *Notebooks*, Hawthorne also pours out his innermost thoughts and the secrets of his heart. To protect the memory of her husband, his wife Sophia destroyed a number of entries before the *Notebooks* were published.

UNFINISHED WORKS

At his death in 1864, Hawthorne left several unfinished novels. These unfinished works were eventually published and include *Septimius Felton* (1872), *The Dolliver Romance* (1876), *Dr. Grimshawe's Secret* (1883), and *The Ancestral Footsteps* (1883).

Septimius Felton, the third of Hawthorne's unfinished novels, was spawned by a story surrounding the house Hawthorne purchased in Concord in 1852 from Bronson Alcott. Henry David Thoreau, a neighbor of Hawthorne, recounted to the latter that many years earlier, there had lived in that same house a man who thought he would never die. Intrigued by

A photograph of Nathaniel Hawthorne, taken near the
end of his life.

the story, Hawthorne tucked it away in his mind where it gestated for several years while he lived abroad. Upon his return to America, he began writing *Septimius Felton*, a romance about a young man who lived during the time of the American Revolution and who sought to discover the secret of living forever. Unfortunately, Hawthorne never completed this novel. It was, however, eventually published as a fragment in 1872, having been edited by Hawthorne's wife Sophia and his daughter Una.

Like *Septimius Felton*, *The Dolliver Romance* echoes the theme of man's search for immortality. In the second attempt to write a novel on this subject, Hawthorne struggled with the advance of old age. Davidson writes:

> But Hawthorne was rapidly growing old. Every day he could feel age creeping more deeply into his bones. Throughout the fall and early winter of 1863 he could barely summon enough strength to climb his favorite hill behind the Wayside and for days on end he sat shivering beside the fire until night came. His hair was turning white; his hands shook with a kind of palsy that made it difficult for him to hold a pen; and, as if the very blood in his body had no more work to do, he was annoyed by frequent nosebleedings.[8]

Hawthorne managed to complete the first install-ment of *The Dolliver Romance* for *The Atlantic Monthly*.

133

However, when the publisher returned the proof sheets, Hawthorne did not even have enough strength to review them.

Afterwards, pushing himself to the limit, he was able to complete two more chapters. In early 1864, however, he admitted that he could not go on:

> I cannot finish it unless a great change comes over me; and if I make too great an effort to do so, it will be my death; not that I should care much for that, if I could fight the battle through and win it, thus ending a life of much smoulder and scanty fire in a blaze of glory. But I should smother myself in mud of my own making.[9]

Thus, *The Dolliver Romance* was also relegated to the realm of Hawthorne's unfinished work.

HAWTHORNE'S LEGACY

Two centuries have passed since Hawthorne penned his works. Even today, they still command much interest. In fact, many of his writings have been made into films. Some have even been performed on the stage.

There are two main reasons that Hawthorne's works are still widely read. The first reason is that he was a literary genius and knew how to write well. The second, and most important, reason is that Hawthorne understood the human heart.

As one of the giants in American literature, Hawthorne continues to command tremendous respect. His works are studied in high schools and universities throughout the world. They are read by fiction lovers everywhere. The reason for his great popularity even in our own day is that Hawthorne wrote about themes that are universal and unchanging. Because of this, he will long hold a prominent place of honor in the world of great literature.

CHRONOLOGY

1804—Born on July 4 in Salem, Massachusetts.

1808—Father, a sea captain, dies in Surinam, Dutch Guinea, as a result of yellow fever. The family is left without financial support and must depend on relatives.

1821–1825—Attends Bowdoin College in Maine. Fellow students include Franklin Pierce (later, President of the United States), Henry Wadsworth Longfellow, and Horatio Bridge. Graduates eighteenth in a class of thirty-eight.

1828—Self-publishes *Fanshawe*, his first novel, anonymously.

1830–1837—Publishes several stories anonymously or pseudonymously in various periodicals. These stories are later collected in *Twice-Told Tales*.

1838—Becomes engaged to Sophia Peabody.

1839–1840—Works in Boston Custom House.

1841—Participates in the Brook Farm Experiment from April to November.

1842–1845—Marries Sophia. The couple lives at the Old Manse in Concord, Massachusetts, and eventually has three children. There,

Hawthorne meets Ralph Waldo Emerson and Henry David Thoreau.

1846–1849—Works as a surveyor in the Salem Custom House. Publishes second collection of short stories called *Mosses from an Old Manse*.

1850—Publishes *The Scarlet Letter*.

1851—Publishes *The House of the Seven Gables*, *The Snow-Image and Other Twice-Told Tales*, and *True Stories from History and Biography*.

1852—Publishes *The Blithedale Romance*, *A Wonder Book for Girls and Boys*, and *The Life of Franklin Pierce*, written for Franklin Pierce's presidential campaign.

1853–1857—Serves as United States Consul to Liverpool. Appointed to this post by President Pierce. Publishes *Tanglewood Tales*.

1857–1859—Lives in Rome and Florence.

1860—Publishes *The Marble Faun*; returns to the United States.

1863—Publishes *Our Old Home: A Series of English Sketches*.

1864—Dies on May 19th at Plymouth, New Hampshire.

CHAPTER NOTES

CHAPTER 1. "THE MAGNETIC CHAIN OF HUMANITY"

1. Nathaniel Hawthorne, "Ethan Brand," *The Complete Novels and Selected Tales of Nathaniel Hawthorne*, ed. Norman Holmes Pearson (New York: Random House, 1937), p. 1194.

2. Nathaniel Hawthorne, *Letter to his mother*, n.d., <http://www.malaspina.com/site/person_615.asp> (July 10, 2003).

3. Nathaniel Hawthorne, *Letter to Henry Wadsworth Longfellow*, June 4, 1837, <http://www.kirjasto.sci.fi/hawthorn.htm> (July 10, 2003).

4. Horatio Bridge, *Personal Recollections of Nathaniel Hawthorne*, 1893, <http://www.eldritchpress.org:8080/nh/hb00.html> (July 10, 2003).

5. Ralph Waldo Emerson, *Journals*, 10:39–40, May 24, 1864, quoted in Edwin Haviland Miller, *Salem Is My Dwelling Place: A Life of Nathaniel Hawthorne* (Iowa City, Iowa: University of Iowa Press, 1991), p. 522.

CHAPTER 2. LIFE IN NEW ENGLAND

1. Robert Spiller, *A Literary History of the United States*, 4th ed., rev. (New York: Macmillan Publishing Co., Inc., 1975), p. 419.

2. Ibid.

3. Ibid.

4. Nathaniel Hawthorne, *"The Scarlet Letter,"* *The Complete Novels and Selected Tales of Nathaniel Hawthorne*, The Modern Library, ed. Norman Holmes Pearson (New York: Random House, 1937), p. 113.

5. Edwin Haviland Miller, *Salem Is My Dwelling Place: A Life of Nathaniel Hawthorne* (Iowa City, Iowa: University of Iowa Press, 1991), p. 17.

6. Ibid., p. 144.

7. Ibid., p. 196.

8. Nathaniel Hawthorne, *"The Blithedale Romance,"* *The Scarlet Letter and The Blithedale Romance* (Boston and New York: Houghton Mifflin Company, 1883), pp. 566–567.

9. Miller, p. 169.

10. Ibid., p. 162.

11. Ibid., p. 163.

12. Ibid., p. 133.

13. Rita K. Gollin, "Figurations of Salem in 'Young Goodman Brown' and 'The Custom-House,'" *Hawthorne in Salem: Scholars Forum*, 2000, <http://www.hawthorneinsalem.com/ScholarsForum/Figurationsof Salem.html> (July 10, 2003).

CHAPTER 3. INFINITE SOLITUDE

1. Nathaniel Hawthorne, *"The Marble Faun,"* *The Complete Novels and Selected Tales of Nathaniel Hawthorne*, The Modern Library, ed. Norman Holmes Pearson (New York: Random House, 1937), p. 655.

2. Leon Edel, *Masters of American Literature*, Shorter Edition, ed. Leon Edel *et al.* (Boston: Houghton Mifflin Company, 1959), p. 472.

3. Henry James, "Nathaniel Hawthorne (1804–1864)," 1896, <http://209.11.144.65/eldritchpress/nh/hjlwbl.html> (July 10, 2003).

4. Edel, p. 474.

5. Nathaniel Hawthorne, *"The Scarlet Letter,"* The *Complete Novels and Selected Tales of Nathaniel Hawthorne*, The Modern Library, ed. Norman Holmes Pearson (New York: Random House, 1937), p. 89.

6. Ibid.

7. John W. Stuart, "Christian Imagery in Hawthorne's *The Scarlet Letter," Hawthorne in Salem, Scholar's Forum*, December 2000, <http://hawthorneinsalem.org/ScholarsForum/MMD1824.html> (July 10, 2003).

8. Ibid.

CHAPTER 4. A ROMANTIC NOVEL

1. Nathaniel Hawthorne, "Preface to *The House of the Seven Gables," The Complete Novels and Selected Tales of Nathaniel Hawthorne*, The Modern Library, ed. Norman Holmes Pearson (New York: Random House, 1937), p. 243.

2. Ibid.

3. C. H. Holman, "Handout by Dr. Roger D. Jones, English 3321," *The Short Story*, Fall 1999, <http://www.english.swt.edu/Jones/hor.html> (July 10, 2003).

4. Nathaniel Hawthorne, *"The Scarlet Letter,"* The *Complete Novels and Selected Tales of Nathaniel Hawthorne*, The Modern Library, ed. Norman Holmes Pearson (New York: Random House, 1937), p. 102.

5. Ibid., p. 103.

6. Ibid.

7. Ibid., p. 115.

8. Ibid., p. 235.

9. Ibid., p. 113.

10. Julian Hawthorne, *"The Scarlet Letter,* by Nathaniel Hawthorne: A Review by Julian Hawthorne," *The Atlantic Monthly*, April 1886, <http://www.theatlantic.com/unbound/classrev/scarlet.htm> (July 10, 2003).

11. Ibid.

12. Nathaniel Hawthorne, *"The Scarlet Letter,"* p. 181.

13. Phyllis Nagy, "The Violence of Civility," *American Theatre*, February 1995, <http://www.questia.com/> (July 4, 2003).

14. Sacvan Bercovitch, *The Puritan Origins of the American Self* (New Haven: Yale University Press, 1975), pp. 176, 242.

15. Julian Hawthorne, *"The Scarlet Letter*, by Nathaniel Hawthorne: A review by Julian Hawthorne."

16. Karen Sanchez-Eppler, "To Be My Own Human Child: Parenting and Romance," *Hawthorne and the Culture of the Family, Panel ALA*, May 2003, <http://hawthorneinsalem.org/ScholarsForum/MMD2037.html> (July 10, 2003).

17. Nathaniel Hawthorne, *"The Scarlet Letter,"* p. 192.

18. Ibid., p. 177.

19. Julian Hawthorne, *"The Scarlet Letter*, by Nathaniel Hawthorne: A review by Julian Hawthorne."

20. Nathaniel Hawthorne, *"The Scarlet Letter,"* p. 179.

CHAPTER 5. HAUNTED BY THE PAST

1. Nathaniel Hawthorne, "Preface to *The House of the Seven Gables," The Complete Novels and Selected Tales of Nathaniel Hawthorne*, The Modern Library, ed. Norman Holmes Pearson (New York: Random House, 1937), p. 243.

2. "Classic Note on *The House of the Seven Gables*," Gradesaver, 1999–2003, <http://www.gradesaver.com/ClassicNotes/Titles/sevengables/shortsumm.html> (July 10, 2003).

3. Claudia Durst Johnson, "The Secular Calling and the Protestant Ethic in *The Scarlet Letter* and *The House of the Seven Gables*," October 20, 2000, <http://hawthorneinsalem.org/ScholarsForum/NEHHawJohnsonlecture.html> (July 10, 2003).

4. Nathaniel Hawthorne, "Preface to *The House of the Seven Gables*," p. 243.

5. Nathaniel Hawthorne, *The House of the Seven Gables*—An Introductory Note," <http://www.americanliterature.com/SG/HOSG1.HTML> (July 10, 2003).

6. Nathaniel Hawthorne, *"The House of the Seven Gables," The Complete Novels and Selected Tales of Nathaniel Hawthorne*, The Modern Library, ed. Norman Holmes Pearson (New York: Random House, 1937), p. 245.

7. Ibid., p. 306.

8. Ibid., p. 315.

9. Ibid.

10. Melissa Pennell, "The Artist and Alienation: Holgrave in *The House of the Seven Gables*, An Introduction," *Hawthorne in Salem*, <http://hawthorneinsalem.org/Literature/AlienationOfTheArtist/Holgrave/Introduction.html> (July 10, 2003).

11. Ibid.

12. Numbers 24:18

13. Nathaniel Hawthorne, *"The House of the Seven Gables,"* p. 396.

14. Ibid., p. 397.

15. Michael Jay Bunker Noble, "Hawthorne's *The House of the Seven Gables," Explicator* 56.2 (1998), pp. 72–73.

CHAPTER 6. FAITH AND SIN

1. Nathaniel Hawthorne, "Young Goodman Brown," *The Complete Novels and Selected Tales of Nathaniel Hawthorne* (New York: Random House, 1937), p. 1033.

2. Ibid.

3. Ibid.

4. Ibid., p. 1034.

5. Ibid.

6. Nathaniel Hawthorne, "The Minister's Black Veil," *The Complete Novels and Selected Tales of Nathaniel Hawthorne*, The Modern Library, ed. Norman Holmes Pearson (New York: Random House, 1937), p. 874.

7. Ibid., p. 873.

8. Ibid.

9. Ibid.

10. Ibid.

11. Ibid., p. 875.

12. Ibid., p. 873.

13. Ibid., pp. 881–882.

CHAPTER 7. CRIMES AGAINST NATURE

1. Thomas St. John, "Dr. Wesselhoeft in 'Rappaccini's Daughter,'" *Nathaniel Hawthorne: Studies in The House of the Seven Gables*, 1993, <http://www.geocities.com/seekingthephoenix/h/hawthorne1.htm> (July 10, 2003).

2. Ibid.

3. Samuel Chase Coale, "The Psychology of Idolatry," *Mesmerism and Hawthorne: Mediums of American Romance* (University of Alabama Press, 1998), p. 56.

4. Michael Colacurcio, *The Province of Piety: Moral History in Hawthorne's Early Tales,* 1984, <http://endeavor.med.nyu.edu/lit-med/lit-med-db/webdocs/webdescrips/hawthorne741-des-.html> (July 10, 2003).

5. Nathaniel Hawthorne, "Rappaccini's Daughter," *The Complete Novels and Selected Tales of Nathaniel Hawthorne*, The Modern Library, ed. Norman Holmes Pearson (New York: Random House, 1937), p. 1059.

6. Ibid., p. 1061.

7. Ibid., p. 1062.

8. Ibid., p. 1065.

9. Laura Stallman, "Survey of Criticism of 'Rappaccini's Daughter' by Nathaniel Hawthorne," *VCU*, 1995, <http://www.vcu.edu/engweb/eng372/rappcrit.htm> (July 10, 2003).

10. Nathaniel Hawthorne, "Ethan Brand," *The Complete Novels and Selected Tales of Nathaniel Hawthorne*, The Modern Library, ed. Norman Holmes Pearson (New York: Random House, 1937), p. 1195.

11. Edwin Haviland Miller, *Salem Is My Dwelling Place: A Life of Nathaniel Hawthorne* (Iowa City, Iowa: University of Iowa Press, 1991), p. 266.

12. Ibid.

13. Mark Harris, "A New Reading of 'Ethan Brand': The Failed Quest," *Studies in Short Fiction*, June 13, 2003 <http://www.questia.com/> (July 10, 2003).

14. Nathaniel Hawthorne, "Ethan Brand," p. 1185.

15. Ibid., p. 1194.

16. Ibid.

17. Ibid.

18. Ibid.

19. Jerry Keen, "The Historical and Present-Day Reality of Ethan Brand's Unpardonable Sin", n.d., <http://www.colin.cc.ms.us/humanities/stories/historical_and_present.htm> (July 10, 2003).

20. Paul Elmer More, "Hawthorne: Looking Before and After." *Nineteenth-Century Literature Criticism*, as cited in Jerry Keen, "The Historical and Present-Day Reality of Ethan Brand's Unpardonable Sin," n.d., <http://www.colin.cc.ms.us/humanities/stories/historical_and_present.htm> (July 10, 2003).

21. Nathaniel Hawthorne, "Ethan Brand," p. 1194.

CHAPTER 8. WAR OF THE HEART AND MIND

1. Nathaniel Hawthorne, "The Birthmark," *The Complete Novels and Selected Tales of Nathaniel Hawthorne*, The Modern Library, ed. Norman Holmes Pearson (New York: Random House, 1937), p. 1022.

2. Ibid., p. 1021.

3. Karen Bernardo, "Nathaniel Hawthorne's 'The Birth-mark'," n.d., <http://www.storybites.com/hawthornebirth.htm> (July 10, 2003).

4. Nathaniel Hawthorne, "The Birthmark," p. 1022.

5. Michael Colacurcio, *The Province of Piety: Moral History in Hawthorne's Early Tales*, (Cambridge, Mass.: Harvard University Press, 1984), p. 251.

6. Ibid., p. 252.

7. William Bradford, *Of Plymouth Plantation: 1620–1647*, (New York: McGraw-Hill, 1981), pp. 219–234.

8. Colacurcio, p. 265.

9. Nathaniel Hawthorne, "The May-Pole of Merrymount," *The Complete Novels and Selected Tales of Nathaniel Hawthorne*, The Modern Library, ed. Norman Holmes Pearson (New York: Random House, 1937), p. 882.

10. Robert L. Gale, *Plots and Characters in the Fiction and Sketches of Nathaniel Hawthorne* (Hamden, Conn.: Archon Books, 1968), p. 107.

11. Nathaniel Hawthorne, "The May-Pole of Merrymount," p. 887.

12. Ibid., p. 889.

13. Colacurcio, p. 251.

14. Donald Connors, *Thomas Morton* (New York: Twayne Publishers, Inc., 1969), p. 126.

15. Nathaniel Hawthorne, "The Artist of the Beautiful," *The Complete Novels and Selected Tales of Nathaniel Hawthorne*, The Modern Library, ed. Norman Holmes Pearson (New York: Random House, 1937), p. 1141.

16. Ibid., p. 1153.

17. Ibid., p. 1154.

18. Ibid., p. 1156.

19. Millicent Bell, *Hawthorne's View of the Artist* (Albany, N.Y.: State University of New York, 1962), p. 114.

20. Ibid., p. 94.

21. Ibid., p. 95.

22. Ibid., pp. 97–98.

23. Randall A. Clack, *The Marriage of Heaven and Earth: Alchemical Regeneration in the Works of Taylor, Poe, Hawthorne, and Fuller* (Westport, Conn.: Greenwood Press, 2000), p. 98.

CHAPTER 9. OLD AND NEW WORLDS

1. Millicent Bell, "*The Marble Faun* and the Waste of History," *Southern Review,* Spring 1999, p. 1.

2. Ibid.

3. Nathaniel Hawthorne, "*The Marble Faun*," *The Complete Novels and Selected Tales of Nathaniel Hawthorne*, The Modern Library, ed. Norman Holmes Pearson (New York: Random House, 1937), p. 603.

4. Ibid., p. 691.

5. Augustus M. Kolich, "Miriam and the Conversion of the Jews in Nathaniel Hawthorne's *The Marble Faun*," *Studies in the Novel*, June 18, 2003 <http://www.questia.com/> (July 10, 2003).

6. Ibid.

7. Ibid.

8. Bell, p. 12.

9. James Russell Lowell, "*The Marble Faun* by Nathaniel Hawthorne: A Review," *The Atlantic Monthly*, April 1860 <http://www.theatlantic.com/unbound/classrev/marblefa.htm> (July 10, 2003).

10. Richard Mezo. "Hawthorne's *The Marble Faun*: A Re-Appraisal." *Dissertation.com*, 1999, <http://www.dissertation.com/library/1120567a.htm> (July 10, 2003).

11. Emily Schiller, "The Choice of Innocence: Hilda in *The Marble Faun*," *Studies in the Novel*, June 18, 2003 <http://www.questia.com/> (July 10, 2003).

12. Mezo.

13. Edwin Haviland Miller, *Salem Is My Dwelling Place: A Life of Nathaniel Hawthorne* (Iowa City, Iowa: University of Iowa Press, 1991), p. 366.

14. Ibid.

15. Ibid., p. 369.

16. Brian Attebery, *The Fantasy Tradition in American Literature: From Irving to Le Guin* (Bloomington, Ind.: Indiana University Press, 1980), p. 43.

17. Hubert H. Hoeltje, *Inward Sky: The Mind and Heart of Nathaniel Hawthorne* (Durham, N.C.: Duke University Press, 1962), p. 235.

18. Mark Y. Hanley, *Beyond a Christian Commonwealth: The Protestant Quarrel with the American Republic, 1830–1860* (Chapel Hill, N.C.: University of North Carolina Press, 1994), p. 121.

19. Nathaniel Hawthorne, "The Celestial Rail-road," *The Complete Novels and Selected Tales of Nathaniel Hawthorne*, The Modern Library, ed. Norman Holmes Pearson (New York: Random House, 1937), p. 1082.

20. Jonathan A. Cook, *Satirical Apocalypse: An Anatomy of Melville's The Confidence-Man* (Westport, Conn.: Greenwood Press, 1996), p. 13.

21. Nathaniel Hawthorne, "My Kinsman, Major Molineux," *The Complete Novels and Selected Tales of Nathaniel Hawthorne*, The Modern Library, ed. Norman Holmes Pearson (New York: Random House, 1937), p. 1209.

22. Peter Shaw, "Their Kinsman, Thomas Hutchinson; Hawthorne, the Boston Patriots, and His Majesty's Royal Governor," *Early American Literature*, XI.2, 1976, p. 183.

23. Nathaniel Hawthorne, "My Kinsman, Major Molineux," p. 1211.

24. Ibid., pp. 1221–1222.

25. Shaw, p. 183.

26. Ibid., p. 184.

27. Nathaniel Hawthorne, "My Kinsman, Major Molineux," p. 1223.

28. Ibid.

29. Mary Jo Bona, *Claiming a Tradition: Italian American Women Writers* (Carbondale, Ill.: Southern Illinois University Press, 1999), p. 38.

30. John Gerlach, *Toward the End: Closure and Structure in the American Short Story* (Montgomery: University of Alabama, 1985), p. 88.

31. Ibid., 106.

32. Stephen R. Portch, *Literature's Silent Language: Nonverbal Communication* (New York: Peter Lang, 1985), p. 47.

CHAPTER 10. CLOSING THE CIRCLE

1. Nathaniel Hawthorne, *Preface to Grandfather's Chair,* <http://www.pagebypagebooks.com/Nathaniel_ Hawthorne/Grandfathers_Chair/Authors_Preface_p1. html> (July 10, 2003).

2. Arlin Turner and Nathaniel Hawthorne, *Hawthorne as Editor: Selections from His Writings in the American Magazine of Useful and Entertaining Knowledge* (Baton Rouge, La.: Louisiana State University Press, 1941), p. 11.

3. Nathaniel Hawthorne, *Grandfather's Chair,* <http://www.pagebypagebooks.com/Nathaniel_Hawth orne/Grandfathers_Chair/Part_I_I_Grandfather_And_ The_Children_And_The_Chair_p1.html> (July 10, 2003).

4. Nathaniel Hawthorne, *Grandfather's Chair,* <http://www.pagebypagebooks.com/Nathaniel_Hawthor ne/Grandfathers_Chair/Part_III_XI_Grandfathers_Drea m_p3.html> (July 10, 2003).

5. Nathaniel Hawthorne, *The English Notebooks,* <http://www.cf.ac.uk/encap/skilton/nonfic/hawthn01. html> (July 10, 2003).

6. Edward Hutchins Davidson, *Hawthorne's Last Phase* (New Haven, Conn.: Yale University Press, 1949), p. 14.

7. Nathaniel Hawthorne, *The American Notebooks,* <http://www.eldritchpress.org/nh/pfanb01.html> (July 10, 2003).

8. Davidson, p. 122.

9. Ibid., p. 123.

GLOSSARY

adultery—Voluntary sexual relations between a married person and someone other than his or her spouse.

allegory—A story expressing a truth about life through the use of symbols.

ambiguity—A literary device that leaves the ultimate meaning of the story up to the reader.

daguerreotypist—A person who engaged in the early photographic process of producing daguerreotype (photographs on a silver or a silver-covered copper plate).

fable—A supernatural story in which animals often speak and act like human beings; a story intended to present a universal truth.

fantasy—A creation of the imagination including bizarre or grotesque characters and settings and often featuring surreal (unnatural or dream-like) events.

faun—A creature of Roman mythology having the legs, hooves, and horns of a goat and the torso and head of a man.

irony—A literary device used to express an idea

that is normally opposite that of the word's literal meaning.

legalism—A philosophy of strict adherence to the letter of the law, even if this means ignoring the original idea or spirit behind the law.

literary device—A formula in writing for producing a certain effect, such as a figure of speech (for example, a metaphor), a narrative style (first person, second person, etc.), or a plot mechanism (such as a flashback).

metaphor—A figure of speech that suggests a comparison or similarity between two normally unrelated things.

novel—A usually long prose narrative that deals with a particular truth of human experience.

original sin—According to certain Christian theology, the state of sin that all humans are born into as a result of the first sin of the first human.

parable—A short story that illustrates a moral attitude or a spiritual principle.

personification—A literary device in which human characteristics are attributed to something that is not human.

Puritan—A Protestant group begun in the sixteenth century that practiced a form of Christianity which emphasized Bible reading, prayer, and preaching in church services. They also stressed self-examination and prayer and believed in the atonement of Christ as the only means of salvation.

quack—Someone who falsely claims to possess medical skill.

romance—A long prose narrative using fantastical happenings in an attempt to connect a bygone era with the present.

Romanticism—An artistic movement of the late eighteenth and early nineteenth centuries which emphasized the imagination and emotions over rational thought.

satire—A literary style in which human behaviors or institutions are held up for ridicule, often through the use of exaggeration, clever humor, and irony.

symbolism—The literary device of using one thing or person to represent another thing or person.

Transcendentalism—A philosophy that taught that man is basically good and that human life went beyond the experience of the senses. The Transcendentalists also believed in the perfectibility of humanity.

utopia—A perfect place; a paradise. The word comes from two Greek words, *ou* meaning "not" or "no," and *topos* meaning "place." The term, therefore, literally means "no place," a place that does not exist.

Major Works by Nathaniel Hawthorne

Novels:

Fanshawe (1828)

The Scarlet Letter (1850)

The House of the Seven Gables (1851)

The Blithedale Romance (1852)

The Marble Faun (1860)

Short Story Collections:

Twice-Told Tales (1837)

Mosses from an Old Manse (1846)

The Snow-Image, and Other Twice-Told Tales (1852)

Other Works:

Grandfather's Chair (1841)

Famous Old People (1841)

Liberty Tree (1841)

Biographical Stories for Children (1842)

True Stories from History and Biography (1851)

A Wonder-Book for Girls and Boys (1852)

The Life of Franklin Pierce (1852)

Tanglewood Tales (1853)

Our Old Home: A Series of English Sketches (1863)

Passages from the American Notebooks (1868)

Passages from the English Notebooks (1870)

The French and Italian Notebooks (1871)

FURTHER READING

Boekhoff, P. M. *The Scarlet Letter*. Farmington Hills, Mich.: The Gale Group, 2003.

Bloom, Harold, ed. *Nathaniel Hawthorne: Comprehensive Research and Study Guide*. Broomall, Pa.: Chelsea House, 1999.

Reynolds, Larry J., ed. *A Historical Guide to Nathaniel Hawthorne*. New York: Oxford University Press, 2001.

Swisher, Clarice, ed. *Readings on Nathaniel Hawthorne*. San Diego: Greenhaven Press, 1996.

Whitelaw, Nancy. *Nathaniel Hawthorne: American Storyteller*. Greensboro, N.C.: Morgan Reynolds, Inc., 2003.

INTERNET ADDRESSES

Nathaniel Hawthorne (1804–1864)
http://www.eldritchpress.org/nh/hawthorne.html

Nathaniel Hawthorne—Biography and Works
http://www.online-literature.com/hawthorne/

Hawthorne in Salem
http://www.hawthorneinsalem.org

Internet Public Library—Online Literary Criticism Collection
http://www.ipl.org.ar/ref/litcrit/

INDEX